Tales of Old Surrey

Tales of
Old Surrey

~

Matthew Alexander
With Illustrations by Don Osmond

COUNTRYSIDE BOOKS
NEWBURY, BERKSHIRE

First Published 1985
Reprinted 1986, 1989, 1992
© Matthew Alexander 1985

COUNTRYSIDE BOOKS
3 CATHERINE ROAD
NEWBURY, BERKSHIRE

ISBN 0 905392 41 8

Designed by Mon Mohan

Produced through MRM Associates Ltd, Reading
Typeset by Acorn Bookwork, Salisbury
Printed in England by J. W. Arrowsmith Ltd., Bristol

To my wife Mary

Contents

SURREY — The map overleaf is by John Speede and shows the county as it was in the early seventeenth century.

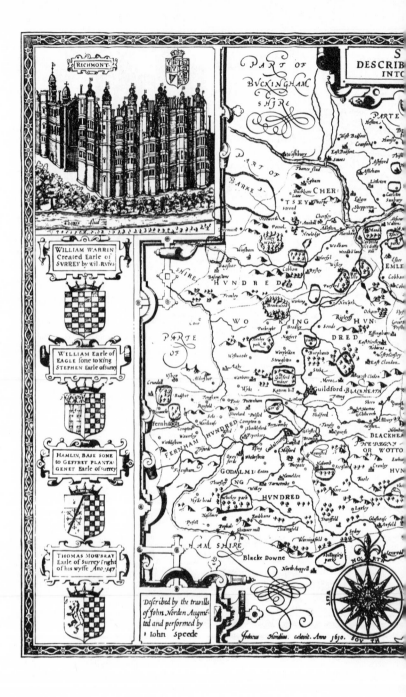

RICHMONT.

S
DESCRIB
INTO

PART OF BVCKINGHAM SHIRE

PART OF BARKE

PARTE

WILLIAM WARREN Created Earle of SVRREY by VVil. RVfVS

WILLIAM Earle of EAGLE fone to King STEPHEN Earle of furry

HAMLIN, BASE fone to GEFFREY PLANTAGENET Earle of furrey

THOMAS MOWBRAY Earle of Surrey i right of his wyffe Ano 1347

PARTE OF

CHER: TSEY

West Beddfont
Crawford
Ashford
Littleton

Washburn
Thames flud
Egham
Buckham Lane
Staines
Thorpe
Trotworth
Chertfey
Pottnol
Annball
Knowledge
Allefton
Hambury

Wodham
Norfol
Iffley
Woodfs land

Efher
EMLE
Cobbam
Co

SHIRE
HVNDRED
Bagfhatt
Frimley
Bafingfton
Cobham
Byfler
Brooky
Working
Pyrford
Ninm'fh
Ockam

WO
KING
DRED
HVN
DRED

PARTE OF

Parbrooke
Bradley
Woodfoe
Mayford
Sende
Ripley
Effingham
Eafthorfleand
Haltons
Weftofcotfley
East Clandon

Onflow
Aldershot
Afhe
Wanborow
Wyke
Katrom hill
Stoughtan
Stoke
Meroc
Weft Claden

Crundell
Badfhot
Tongham
Rouftfold
Sete
Marchant
Poole Puttenham
Littleton
Titting
Shere
Lo: Martin
Chilworth
Albury
Holmhw

Fernham
Compton
Waverley
Worththam
Compton
fhold
fhuldfford
Pyperhars
Fernombe
Brasmley
Jangly
Wanfell
Peafmarfh

Guildford BLACKHEATH
Shalford

FERNHAM HVNDRED

Tilford

Oxens ford
Whelefreta
Milford
Godalming
Borgate
Nafembt

Elftead
Farncombe
Brogate
Nafembt
Ficleland

BLACKHEA
THE REGNI
OR WOTTO
HVN

Fitenham
GODALMI: Enten
Thurfley NG
Wilfey

Hameldn
Farnombty
Cranley
Knole
Lovley

Hyde head
Whitley park
Hafelmer

HVNDRED

Hafelmer
Peffell
Popbal
Shoatcr mill
Chidmefild

Dunfold
Glafhoufe
Anfold

Warningfeld

Loxley

HAM SHIRE
Blacke Downe
North chappell

Bullingfhig
park

NO:
RTH

Jov
VIY

Described by the travills of Iohn Norden Augmented and performed by i Iohn speede

Iodocus Hondius celavit Anno 1610.

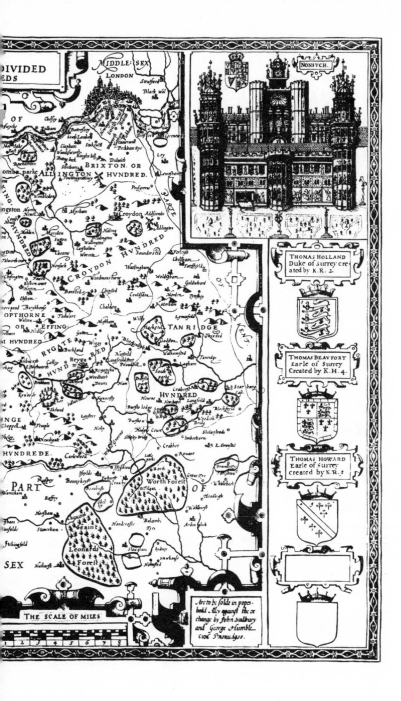

DIVIDED
EDS

MIDDLE·SEX
LONDON

NONSVCH

Stratford
Black wal

OF

Chelsy

Battersey
South Lambeth
Clapham
Wandsworth
Knights hill
Stretham

Streamwell
Drysleys
Peckham Rye

Greenwych

Dulwich

BRIXTON. OR
HVNDRED.

Ley

Lugham

ombe park
ALLINGTON HVNDRED.

Humbledon

Proserow

SARE

ngton
Camb
ville
Mylden

Mytcham

Croydon Addiscombe

HVNDRED

INGTON
HVNDRED

Morden
Nevill

Sutton

Haling

Wallington
Leysham

Alington

Chrame

Woocote

Saunders led

Ferleigh

HVNDRED

Malde
Dune

Mordon

Nonsuch

CROYDON HVNDRED

Chelsham

Tatffeild

Talworth court

Woodmans Furm

Warmingham

Woldesham

Goldsworh

OPTHORNE

Banstid

Chipsted

Couldston

Morden

Fryshey

Esham

Chaldon

Lymesfeild

Ketersham

ore and Burghouse

Tadworth

Meysham

OR · EFFING
M HVNDRED

Walton

Fetley

Gatton

Blackfeild

Markstead

TANRIDGE

Godston

Oxsted

RYGATE HVND RED

Buckland

Witgy

Nutfeild

Walhamsford

Tanridge

Reygat

Kingsfeild fret

Laghan

Brockham

Bletchworth

Ricsagelsha

Powdsell

South
park

Star bury
East

Bayle
park

Crabnest

Horne

Newchch

Longfeild

PART OF KENT

Skloed

Loysret

Ham

Horsley

Burstolodge

Hodeshcourt

Godsick
Bride

Blockfeild

Shelenybrooke

Bastow

Imberborn

ChaPPell

Temple

Newhgate

Crabbet

Rouant

Little
park

R L Grovstd

HVNDREDE.

Carlewood

Brambry
Mershton

Starbury

W halebech

Resfry

Iesolde

ferhurst

Worth

Grews Tye

Hoodleigh

PART

Resfry
Warnham

Bonnykey

Besubush

Crawly

OF

W ahhorst

Horsham

Shipston

Seaint

Handcrosse

Balssmb

Ardinghch

Sham
imsfolde

Stanwham

Leonards

Slaugham

Tye

Forest

Sydney

SEX

Nuthurst

Nuthurst

Southouse

Are to be solde in popes-
head Alley against the ex
change by Iohn Sudbury
and George Humble
cum Priuilegio.

THE SCALE OF MILES

1 2 3 4 5 6 7 8

THOMAS HOLLAND
Duke of Surrey cre-
ated by K.R. 2.

THOMAS BEAVFORT
Earle of Surrey
Created by K.H. 4.

THOMAS HOWARD
Earle of Surrey
created by K.R. 3.

The Alchemist
of Stoke

Throughout history the lure of gold has led people on to every possible kind of foolishness. In particular, the notion that cheap, base metals could be turned into gold by a magical 'Philosopher's Stone' has enticed generations of men to spend their lives in pursuit of this ever-elusive substance. Many of these alchemists claimed that theirs was a mystical, philosophic quest for truth, but there is no doubt that others were simply looking for a way of getting rich quickly. The fact that none ever succeeded — or none ever succeeded without trickery — did nothing to deter others from trying where their predecessors had failed. The story of the Alchemist of Stoke, however, has a number of unusual features. Firstly, he lived, not in the superstitious Middle Ages, but in the Age of Reason, when science was beginning to illuminate man's knowledge of his world. Again, he was a wealthy young man, well-educated and with good prospects, not a confidence trickster needing to swindle a gullible public for a living. The motives that drove him on in his short life — and to his tragic end — will never be known for certain.

James Higginbottom was born in London in 1752 and graduated from Oxford when he was 25. In 1781, however, something happened that was to change his life utterly. His uncle, James Price, died, leaving him a fortune on the understanding that he adopted the surname of Price. And so it came to pass that the wealthy young James Price, M.A., bought a small country estate in Surrey, at Stoke, just to the north of Guildford. In his house he set up a well-equipped laboratory, intending to devote much of his time to his hobby of chemistry. He sufficiently impressed the established scientists of his day to be elected a Fellow of the Royal Society, the foremost scientific society in the land.

His researches, however, were out of keeping with the spirit of the age. The new scientific reasoning relied only on observable facts, not the unsupported theories of ancient writers. Price, on the other hand, eagerly read the books of the old alchemists, and convinced himself that they contained an element of truth. In particular, he thought that mercury, silver, and gold were all forms of the same substance, and that a suitable catalyst would transform one into the other. This catalyst, of course, was none other than the ancient alchemists' 'Philosopher's Stone'. Price set to work, and within a year he claimed to have discovered the secret in the form of two powders — a white one which turned mercury into silver, and a red one which turned mercury or silver into gold. He revealed his discovery to an astonished world in May 1782, by holding a series of demonstrations witnessed by increasing numbers of the local gentry and nobility. Various substances were heated with mercury in a crucible, the magic powder added, and, before the very eyes of the onlookers, small amounts of gold or silver were produced. Price insisted on having a sealed sample of the gold analysed — and sure enough it was found to be pure, genuine gold. However, his eagerness to prove there was no trickery might itself have aroused suspicions, just as a conjuror's reassuring patter never convinces the audience entirely.

Not surprisingly, the experiments caused a sensation; first around Guildford, then in London, then throughout the country. The King himself, George III, personally inspected and approved specimens of the wonderful gold, and in July James Price M.A. was made Dr. Price by his university. However, sceptics and cynics were soon pouring doubt on his results — and his motives. When he published an account of his experiments later in the year, Price felt obliged to answer his critics. No deceit was possible in front of such reliable witnesses, he claimed, nor did he stand to make any money personally; not only did it cost him £17 to make £4 worth of gold, in any case he already had all the money he needed. But he obstinately refused to reveal the composition of the magical powders — and his secrecy annoyed everyone.

Those who believed him thought he was selfish; those who did not, thought he was a crook. His friends — and they were getting fewer — urged him to tell the truth, and suggested that he might have been innocently mistaken by using mercury bought from gilders and so contaminated with gold. Price refused to admit he was wrong, however, and promised a full explanation — which never appeared.

Resentment of his attitude was felt nowhere more keenly than in the Royal Society, whose reputation was being tarnished by the young charlatan. The President, the formidable Sir Joseph Banks, summoned Price and demanded that he repeat his experiments in front of expert scientists — or face expulsion from the Society and disgrace. Dr. Price returned to Guildford early in 1783 to prepare a fresh series of experiments — and to make his will. He seems to have spent the next few months in despair. He must surely have known all along that his claims were at best mistaken, at worst fraudulent, and that inevitably he would be exposed. Eventually he invited a deputation from the Royal Society to his house at Stoke and on 3rd August 1783, three respected scientists arrived to witness the controversial experiments with their own critical eyes. Dr. Price welcomed them and led them to his laboratory, where he invited them to inspect the apparatus. As they bent over the crucibles and furnaces the three chemists heard a gasp and a thud behind them. Spinning round, they saw Price lying at their feet, an empty bottle of prussic acid in his hand. He was stone dead.

So ended the short but remarkable career of the Alchemist of Stoke. The inquest judged him insane, and so not guilty of suicide — there was also a suggestion that he had mistaken the poison for brandy. In any event, he was entitled to Christian burial, and this he received in St. John's church nearby. The memorial tablet to him is still to be seen above the south door. Ironically, it gets both the date of his death and his age wrong, but the short Latin epitaph is appropriate, whatever kind of man may he have been. — Dr. James Price, F.R.S. – 'Heu! qualis erat' – 'Alas, what a fellow he was', or alternatively 'Oh, how mistaken he was!'

The Hindhead
Murder

On the afternoon of Sunday 24th September 1786 a sailor was walking to Portsmouth along the turnpike from Godalming. This was not an unusual sight, for sailors paid off at Portsmouth often went up to London to spend their accumulated money and returned to find another ship. Often they would hire a coach to make the journey up but nearly always they would have to walk back, their money all spent on drink and riotous living. This particular sailor was unusual in that he still had some money left in his pockets. Enough, in the event, to cost him his life.

He decided to rest and refresh himself and on entering a pub at Mousehill, just beyond Milford, he found three other sailors already there. One of them he recognised as a former shipmate and they fell into conversation. It turned out that all three — Michael Casey, James Marshall, and Edward Lonegan — were unemployed and short of money. Their new companion reassured them. He had plenty of money and would pay for the drinks. As he pulled out a golden guinea to pay the landlord, the others' eyes must have gleamed with envy. The sailor proposed that all four should walk on to Portsmouth together, and he would pay the reckoning on the way. Perhaps mere friendship prompted him, or perhaps he thought he would be safer in company on the lonely road.

The four set out, but had only covered a little over two miles before they felt the need for more refreshment and stopped at the Red Lion, Thursley. Once more the kind companion paid for the round of drinks. They then set off up the steep road that climbed to the very top of Hindhead, which in those days was the road running south from Thursley past the church. At the top they paused to regain their breath. Perhaps the generous sailor turned his back on his new companions for a moment to gaze around at the wild landscape falling away into the Devil's Punchbowl at his feet. Without warning he was struck a blow on the head that knocked him to the ground. The three assailants drew their knives and, as they had secretly agreed beforehand, each made two cuts in the unfortunate victim's throat. One wished to make absolutely certain. 'Lend me your knife. I'll have another cut at him.' The head was very nearly severed from the body. Emptying the pockets, they stripped the corpse and dragged it some two hundred yards down into the Devil's Punchbowl. They then climbed back up onto the Portsmouth Road and continued on their way.

They were not unobserved. Two workmen saw them dump the body and were horrified by what they found when they hurried over to the spot. Night was falling, however, and neither felt like tackling the three thugs unassisted. They went back to Thursley for help, and with eight or nine others set off in pursuit of the murderers. They caught up with them at a pub at Rake, near Petersfield, trying to sell their victim's clothes. The three were arrested and taken back to the scene of their crime. Each in turn was forced to touch the body; there was a superstition that a murdered corpse bleeds at the touch of its killer. The result of this is not recorded, although one of the prisoners broke down and wept. The others showed no emotion and claimed they would do as much again. They were taken to Justice Fielding of Haslemere and committed to Guildford Gaol.

The identity of the murdered man was never established and so no relatives could be informed to arrange the burial. However, the savage crime had shocked the district and a public subscription paid for the funeral plus an elaborate gravestone in Thursley churchyard recording the circumstances of the horrible deed. Casey, Marshall, and Lonegan were tried for murder at the next Assizes at Kingston and, after confessing their guilt, were condemned to death. On 17th April 1787 they returned once more to the top of Hindhead, where they were hanged by the neck until they were dead. The bodies were then soaked in tar as a preservative and riveted into iron frames which were hung from the gibbet. This was a wooden post thirty feet high with an iron wheel fixed horizontally on the top. The bodies of the criminals hung from the rim of the wheel by chains, swinging and groaning in the wind as an awful warning to passing travellers.

Soon after the execution a stone was put up at the scene of the murder by the owner of the land, James Stilwell of Cosford House, with an inscription commemorating the crime. In 1826 the trustees of the turnpike decided to make the road over Hindhead safer and easier by cutting a new route further down the hillside. They had the memorial stone moved down to a spot beside the new road, but this liberty enraged the donor's heir, John Hawkins. He had it removed, and a replacement put up by the trustees was vandalised. Hawkins later restored the original stone to the original spot, adding an inscription 'Cursed be the man who injureth or removeth this stone'. As it happened, it was ultimately moved again to the site which it now occupies on the hillside above the present road that skirts the Devil's Punchbowl.

This beautiful spot had acquired such a morbid reputation that in 1851 Sir William Erle felt that something of a more uplifting nature was required. He had a large granite cross, inscribed with suitable expressions of Christian forgiveness and repentance. He was under the impression that the cross was on the site of the gibbet, which had rotted away by this time. In fact he was mistaken. It stood some way away on the very summit of the hill. The gibbet is gone, but the cross, the memorial stone and the gravestone in Thursley churchyard bear ample witness to a cruel and ungrateful crime, and a swift and grisly retribution.

The Bleeding Stone
and the
Buckland Shag

A mile or so west of Reigate the road from Dorking crosses a shallow stream. Today the road is busy with motor traffic but many years ago, according to legend, it was a silent and lonely spot — the scene of a poignant tragedy and a terrifying haunting.

The story is told of how a farmer's beautiful daughter was courted by the son of the squire. One evening they were walking together beside the stream and halted by a large stone that stood there. The young man talked earnestly to the girl, making a most improper suggestion. She, shocked beyond description when she realised what he was proposing, fell dead at his feet. The would-be seducer was then seized by remorse at the result of his wickedness, and, drawing out a dagger, stabbed himself through the heart. In the morning their bodies were found side-by-side — and the nearby stone trickling with blood. No wiping or cleaning could stem the flow, and it continued to bleed as a grim reminder of the tragedy.

It is unclear how this tale is connected with the dreadful monster which is also said to have haunted this spot. This was the Buckland Shag, a fearsome four-footed beast like an ape with a shaggy coat. It was supposed to squat upon the Bleeding Stone at midnight, beside the stream which still bears the name Shag Brook. It was indeed a brave villager who dared to pass that way at night, but one such was the Buckland man who was spending a convivial evening in an ale-house in Reigate after attending the day's market. A drinking companion brought up the unpleasant thought that he would have to pass by the Shag's lair on his way home. The ale made the Buckland man brave, and he swore that if the Shag appeared, he would fight it off with his trusty hawthorn stick. At length the time came to leave the cheery warmth and company of the pub and he ventured out into the darkness for the lonely walk home. As he trod the path across the meadow near the brook, the Shag suddenly appeared in front of him. True to his word, the villager struck out with his stick, which landed with a hollow sound 'as upon a blanket'. In an instant he became stone cold sober, and was overcome by a sudden panic. He fled as fast as his legs could carry him, over the stile and the fields that lay between him and safety. Close behind he could hear the Shag pursuing him and it was only when he collapsed inside his cottage door that the terrible figure vanished. What the story does not tell us, however, is whether his drinking-companion had left the pub before he did, and whether he was carrying a blanket at the time . . .

Horses are very sensitive animals and it is well known that they can feel presences that humans cannot. In about 1800 a team of four horses was returning to Reigate one night after delivering a waggon-load of corn to Dorking. As they came to the stone beside Shag Brook they suddenly halted. No amount of yelling and whipping by the waggoners, or even pushing, would get the horses to take another step forward. Sweating and trembling with fear, they eventually had to be unharnessed and led away. When day broke, a single horse was able to pull the empty waggon across the brook that four could not — or would not — cross the night before.

Another drunken wager led to a further fearsome encounter. A cavalry trooper was billeted in a nearby pub and, while drinking one night with the locals, heard them speak in awed voices about the monstrous Shag, how it perched on the Bleeding Stone at midnight and could make itself invisible. The soldier laughed at the bumpkins, and laid a bet that he would ride his horse at midnight past the stone and back to the pub. At the appointed hour he set out, and passed the stone without anything to disturb his happy contemplation of the easy money he was going to make. He rode a little further, then wheeled his mount round to make

his way back. As soon as he reached the stone once more, he felt an invisible form leap up behind him and clutch him round the waist. The horse shuddered and bolted, and the trooper dug in his spurs, all ale-courage evaporated. The unseen thing still clung to him as he urged his terrified animal on, and it was not until the welcome lights of the ale-house came into view ahead that the dreadful grip was relaxed. The trooper arrived at the pub rather faster than he had left it, and his obvious terror and exhaustion may have given a certain grim satisfaction to the villagers as they handed over his winnings. Not for a thousand times the money, he said, would he ever go that way at midnight again.

Modern-day travellers need not fear, however. The spot, it is generally agreed, is no longer haunted. By the early 1800s the lord of the manor ordered the stone to be removed and taken to his own grounds as a way of quieting the superstitious fears of his tenants. As for the Buckland Shag, that fearsome monster is to be seen no more, for did not the vicar of Buckland himself exorcise it? With bell, book, and candle, the Shag was ceremoniously banished — supposedly to the Red Sea. There is, however, a disturbing report of a lane at Cranleigh being haunted by a creature called 'Buck-me-shag'. Could it be that the 'Buckland Shag' was only driven a mere dozen miles from its old haunt?

The Myth of the Pilgrims' Way

It would be hard to think of an historical notion more widely held in Surrey, and more cherished, than that of the Pilgrims' Way. A trackway is pictured, running along the sand ridge to the south of the Downs right through the heart of the county. Along this there streams a throng of mediaeval travellers, picturesquely attired in hooded gowns, with staves in their hands — or perhaps the wealthier on horseback, telling each other tales to while away the weary journey. All are hurrying to the shrine of St. Thomas à Becket in Canterbury Cathedral, where the archbishop had been murdered in 1170. He became the most popular English saint, and stories of miracles attracted thousands to his shrine with offerings and prayers. Surely, many would come from the west, through Winchester — and what more natural than to travel directly along the line of the downs to Canterbury? This romantic image had great appeal for the Victorians, obsessed with those Middle Ages they so revered but so little understood, and has continued to the present day with no signs of dimming. Yet there is no evidence that a single mediaeval pilgrim ever went along the Pilgrims' Way.

The theory was first thought up in the middle of the last century by a Kentish antiquarian with the splendidly appropriate name of Albert Way. He interpreted a few dubious place-names as evidence of such a route and was apparently so enchanted by his 'discovery' that he ignored the obvious inconsistencies. Albert Way's ideas would probably not have gained much attention, however, had it not been for the Ordnance Survey and Captain Edward Renouard James. He was a Royal Engineer map-maker, and while surveying Surrey in the 1860s he enthusiastically accepted the 'Pilgrims' Way' as fact, and traced what he thought was its course on his maps (a course which has been modified at several points by later Pilgrims' Wayfarers). He also published, in 1871, a booklet which not only put forward the theory but elaborated it to an almost farcical extent. He even went as far as to suggest that John Bunyan walked the Way, and had based scenes in *The Pilgrim's Progress* on places and events along it. All this despite the facts that Bunyan almost certainly never entered Surrey in his life, lived a hundred years after the pilgrimages had ceased, and belonged to a Protestant sect that would have considered earthly pilgrimages to saints' shrines as dangerously superstitious. Few of his readers, however, commented on the lack of solid proof that Captain James offered. Most accepted his romantic notions as if they were historical facts. The reason for this is not hard to find — it was an age which, faced with a choice between the romantic and the historical, invariably chose the romantic. Later writers elaborated on the theme. Many of the houses built near the route were christened with suitable 'pilgrimy' names, and local magazines have run articles at intervals ever since, charting the supposed course of the Way and expanding on its supposed history. Perhaps most bizarre of all is the plaque erected in 1936 at St. Catherine's ferry stating 'You who pass by . . . are treading the path trod by Geoffrey Chaucer's Canterbury pilgrims.' If any pilgrim journeyed from Southwark to Canterbury via Guildford, it must have been because of the ale he drank at the Tabard.

The 'Pilgrims' Way' idea fails the test on two vital points: firstly that it was a continuous track from Winchester to Canterbury, and secondly that it was ever used by pilgrims. The fact that different routes were suggested at different places by different writers emphasises the disjointed nature of the supposed trackway. The 'Pilgrims' Way' is nothing more than a series of disconnected tracks along a series of hills, rather than a continuous ridge. These would have existed in the Middles Ages, but would have been short, local paths rather than a cross-country route. Again, mediaeval records make no mention of pilgrims using the route — an astonishing omission if it had genuinely been used by the hoards that have been imagined. It simply was not a recognised cross-country route. For example, Chaucer's shipman, from Dartmouth in the West Country, sensibly travelled via London, where inns were available to receive him, rather than make a difficult cross-country journey through the underpopulated wasteland of central Surrey.

There is a saying among local historians that 'bad history drives out good' in the sense that the brightly-coloured, romantic myth will always be preferred to the dull, often fragmentary fact. The scholar has often to say 'we do not, we can never know — the records simply do not survive — we must accept that there will always be gaps in our knowledge of the past.' For many of us, perhaps for most, this is highly unsatisfactory, when a little imagination can fill in the gaps — and in the colours of our own choosing. Those that follow, however, may not be able to distinguish where the facts end and the myth begins. Many people may be surprised to find the truth of the 'Pilgrims' Way' questioned; some may even resent the fact that it has been. They should rest assured, however. The idea of the 'Pilgrims' Way' has become so firmly established in the minds of the people of Surrey that it will never be uprooted merely by historical fact.

The Telegraph and
the Semaphore

I n the middle of the 1790s Britain was at war with revolutionary France, and the Royal Navy was once more charged with defending our shores and carrying the war to the enemy. The Navy was controlled by the Admiralty in London, but all its major ports were many miles from the capital. Orders and reports had to travel to and from the coast at the speed a man could ride. It regularly took a horseman six or seven hours to cover the 70 miles from London to the nation's main naval base at Portsmouth, and although this could be cut to as little as 4½ hours in a desperate emergency, this was still considered dangerously slow when only the fastest of responses could protect England from a French invasion. A quicker means of communication was needed, and it was found in the form of the telegraph.

A telegraph is a chain of hilltop stations that signal to each other visually. Strictly speaking, a semaphore is a kind of telegraph that uses pivoted arms, but the two terms were often confused at the time — and subsequently. The Chappe brothers had already introduced a semaphore network in France. In England, though, the Reverend Lord George Murray, fourth son of the Duke of Atholl, invented a different system: the shutter telegraph. This consisted of a wooden hut with a twenty-foot framework above it, in which hung six wooden boards or shutters about five feet square. They pivoted in sockets on either side and could be swung open or closed by pulling ropes in the hut below. Sixty-three different combinations of open and closed shutters were possible, spelling out all the letters and numbers and also pre-arranged words and even complete sentences. By watching the shutters of the next station up the line through a telescope,

23

the signal could be repeated as it was spelt out and so passed on to the next station down the line. Murray was paid £2,000 for his invention and in 1795 an experimental line to Chatham was begun. George Roebuck was appointed as engineer and work on the Portsmouth telegraph began early the following year. Ten stations were built: Admiralty to Chelsea, then Putney Heath to Cabbage Hill between Ashtead and Oxshott, from there to Netley Heath on the Downs above Gomshall, then Hascombe Hill to Blackdown from whence two others on Beacon Hill and Portsdown relayed the signals to Portsmouth. Each station had a crew of four. Two would keep a watch on the stations before and after them in the line, and two would stand by the ropes. When a message began to be spelled out at the next station up, the man at the telescope that side called out the figures and the appropriate ropes were hauled to repeat them. The man on the other telescope checked that the next station down the line was copying them correctly. Of course, if a message was to pass in the other direction, the two telescope men simply swapped jobs. In this way a single-character signal could be passed from London to Portsmouth in less than a minute — and in fact this was done every day to synchronise the ships' navigational chronometers with the Time Ball at Greenwich. Or rather, it would have been done every day in ideal conditions. Rain and fog frequently closed the telegraph down, and experiments with lanterns failed to solve the problem of signalling at night. Nevertheless, the shutter telegraph was a great help in the war against Napoleon — and when he was sent into exile in 1814 the war ended and with it the reason for the telegraph. After all, it had only been intended as a temporary measure, and the flimsy hilltop huts cannot have been abandoned by their crews with much reluctance. The line closed in September 1814, but seven months later Napoleon returned to France and war was renewed. The shutters were quickly set to work again and it was not until March 1816, nine months after the victory at Waterloo, that they were abandoned for ever.

However, the Lords of the Admiralty had found the telegraph very useful during its twenty-year 'temporary' operation, and decided to build a permanent network. An improved system was

needed, though, and after experiments they adopted the device invented by Rear Admiral Sir Home Popham. Popham was a distinguished seaman with a somewhat buccaneering reputation and like Murray, he was paid £2,000 for his signalling improvements. Popham's telegraph was a true semaphore, with two 8 foot pivoting arms, one above the other on a 30 foot mast. The waving arms could spell out 48 separate characters, enough for all the letters and numbers and some pre-arranged codes. The arms needed only one man to work them and were easier to make out at a distance than the shutters, although the arms needed to be seen silhouetted against the sky. This meant some of the masts would have to be built on towers. In 1818 Thomas Goddard was employed to survey the route, and he and his men spent months struggling up wild hillsides with ladders, telescopes, and portable semaphores to work out the best sites for the stations. The route finally adopted diverged from the old shutter line at Putney Heath, running to Kingston Hill, Telegraph Hill between Hinchley Wood and Claygate, Chatley Heath between Ockham and

25

Cobham, then to Pewley Hill at Guildford, Bannicle Hill near Witley, and Haste Hill at Haslemere. Six stations in Hampshire completed the link to Portsmouth. The new semaphore was finished in June 1822 and 3 years later a line from the Admiralty to Plymouth was planned. This would have shared the Portsmouth line up to Chatley Heath, where it branched westwards to a tall tower next to Worplesdon church, and then to a station on the Hog's Back above Tongham, where the Hog's Back Hotel now stands. Popham's semaphore was an improvement on Murray's shutters, but still the weather prevented signalling on an average of one day in three. The invention of the electric telegraph spelled out the death warrant of the semaphore. Here was a system that operated instantaneously, whatever the weather, at all hours of the day and night — and without the expense of employing teams of signallers. The London & South Western Railway constructed an electric telegraph alongside its track to Gosport in 1844 and the semaphore was closed down at the end of 1847.

Nothing remains of the wooden huts of the shutter telegraph, but there are still traces of the semaphores. The stations at Claygate and on Pewley Hill, Guildford have been converted to houses, the latter having a dome added to the tower, and the Haslemere Station has been incorporated in the Whitwell Hatch Hotel. The station that has survived with least alteration, though, is the tall octagonal tower on Chatley Heath. Its mast and arms have gone, but it is still an impressive monument to the days when telegraphs connected London, through Surrey, to the sea.

Curious Charities

It has been a long-established custom for wealthy people to leave money in their wills for charitable purposes. Usually land or some other property would be left in trust, or money invested, the income to be spent on carefully specified purposes. Often these charities were purely religious, for example, towards repairs to the parish church, or paying for a clergyman to preach a sermon on a certain day each year. Occasionally the money went for public works such as the upkeep of roads and bridges. The vast majority, though, went to the poor. Before the state began to take over responsibility for the old, the sick, and the unemployed their only hope was the generosity of their wealthier neighbours.

Most of the old Surrey charities provided money, food, fuel, or clothing for the poor. Often, though, this was limited by the terms of the wills to a certain number of people and on only one or two days every year. The character of the recipients was also carefully specified, the donor usually drawing a rigid distinction between those incapable of supporting themselves and those quite able, but unwilling. Often church attendance was required as a condition of receiving the charity, and as the trustees were usually the churchwardens they would be well able to keep an eye on any backsliders. Each stage of the pauper's life was provided for: charity schools for poor children were widespread, and there were funds to apprentice young men to a trade or provide a marriage portion for a maid. After a lifetime supported by one or another benefaction, the old pauper might be lucky enough to be accommodated in one of the many almshouses that were such a feature of Tudor and Jacobean Surrey — Abbot's Hospital at Guildford and Whitgift's at Croydon being perhaps the most imposing. Do not imagine, however, that more than a small number of the many poor people benefited from these charities. For most, life was a constant struggle.

Amidst this catalogue of rather dour do-gooding, it is refreshing to come across the benefaction of Thomas Kemp, who in 1730 left £1 to Chertsey and 10 shillings to East Molesey for 'the young men of the parish to ring and make merry with on the 6th of August yearly, in rememberance of the donor.' This was a most generous sum, enough to provide the bell ringers with a good dinner and more ale, perhaps, than was advisable. Sadly, Thomas Kemp's benevolence is now forgotten and the 6th of August — his birthday, perhaps? — now passes unmarked. His charity was not the only one of its kind, however; the Witley ringers did even better after a land deal in 1682 brought them 30 shillings a year. Reigate church even had a plot of land, known as Crab Tree Field, the rent from which was intended to pay for new bell-ropes.

When writing their wills, the benefactors would sometimes go into the most minute details concerning their charities — the exact cut of the gowns to be given away, or even the recipe for the beef broth to be doled out. Few though were as elaborately precise as William Glanville, who died in 1717 and is buried in Wotton churchyard. He stipulated that every year £2 should be divided among five poor boys under the age of 16 who, with their hands on his tombstone, could recite from memory the Apostles' Creed, the Ten Commandments, and the Lord's Prayer; read the 15th chapter of the First Epistle to the Corinthians, and write out two verses from it. It is one of the unfortunate results of inflation in the present century that the sums of money specified in such charities have become almost worthless. Glanville's charity, for example, was last claimed in about 1980 and candidates are hard to find. Few young men are willing today to put themselves to so much trouble for so little.

One philanthropist above all others, however, gave sums of money to the poor that are impressive even by modern standards. Henry Smith laid out many thousands of pounds to all the towns and villages of Surrey, and even more remarkably he gave much of it during his lifetime. Little is known about Smith himself. He was born in Wandsworth (then, of course, part of Surrey) in 1548 and died in 1627. He may have been a silversmith, but whatever his business it was certainly profitable, for he was able to give £1,000 to each of the major towns in his county — Croydon, Dorking, Farnham, Godalming, Guildford, and Kingston. He may simply have forgotten about Reigate until he came to write his will, for he left the town a similar amount and the bulk of his immense fortune to the other parishes of Surrey. The tale is often repeated that Henry Smith was an eccentric millionaire who wandered the country lanes dressed as a beggar, with his dog at his heels. 'Dog Smith' is the nickname later foisted on him, and the story goes on to relate how he was once whipped as a vagabond in one Surrey parish and so never left it a penny in his will. A good tale, but utterly untrue, because every single parish in Surrey benefited from his extraordinary generosity.

Of all the charities of Surrey, though, the most picturesque is Dicing for the Maid's Money. In 1674 John How left £400 to be invested, the interest from it to be paid to a maid-servant who had served for two years with good character within the old borough of Guildford. Two suitable candidates were to be selected, they would throw dice, and the maid who threw highest won the money. The loser could try again for the next two years. However, the practice was adopted of giving the loser the money left by John Parsons for apprentices, if it remained unclaimed. It happens that the apprentice's money is actually more than the maid's — so now the winner loses and the loser wins.

Dicing for the Maid's Money still goes on each year, but it is increasingly difficult to find candidates. Not only has the value of money changed; so has our way of life and living-in servants are hard to find. Nevertheless, despite Victorian rationalisation and the growth of the Welfare State, a few of our old and unusual charities have not been forgotten and we still remember the benefactors who founded them when this was a very different land.

Shrove Tuesday in Dorking

Shrove Tuesday, the day before the fast of Lent begins, was marked by a number of traditional observances as a kind of last fling before the austere days ahead. Pancakes were eaten, of course, and certain games played, such as throwing sticks at tethered cockerels. The most spectacular game, though, was street football. This was played in many of the towns of northern Surrey in the early years of the last century, most notably at Kingston-upon-Thames, where it attracted spectators — and players — from a wide area of London.

The rules of street football in Surrey were very simple. Any number could play, the two sides usually represented one half of the town against the other, and the ball was kicked off or thrown in at a central spot at a fixed time. The winners were the side who could get the ball to their own goal (often a stream) or who held the ball in their own half of the town at the hour set for finishing. Apart from this, the players could do as they pleased. Actually kicking the ball became rarer as the numbers playing increased and carrying — 'hugging' — the ball became more common. Any kicking done in the huge scrums that resulted was usually directed at opponents' shins. The fact that this all took place in the main streets of the town meant that the shops had to be closed and barricaded against the powerful crush of the crowd. This contributed to a change of attitude towards Shrove Tuesday football by the beginning of Queen Victoria's reign. Whereas previously many of the shopkeepers and leading tradesmen of the towns had actively supported and played the game, now they were increasingly reluctant to lose an afternoon's business — and were increasingly alarmed by the disorderly working-class mob.

Local councils attempted to put an end to the tradition, but it was only with the introduction of the police force in the 1830s that they had effective means to carry this out. At Kingston, for example, massive police reinforcements were drafted into the town on Shrove Tuesday 1867 and the game was stopped amid riotous scenes. As the century drew on, Shrove Tuesday football was banished from the streets of one Surrey town after another, until there was only one survivor at Dorking.

Dorking lies in the very centre of the county, away from the suburban towns near London, and this is possibly why the game lingered longest here. It is uncertain when street football began at Dorking, probably in the mid 1830s, but it quickly became established as a tradition and continued until the early years of the present century.

The day's festivities were heralded in the morning by a bizarre group that paraded the town, led by a man carrying a pole with a cross-bar from the ends of which hung two — and later three — painted footballs. On the cross-bar was painted the slogan

31

'wind and water's Dorking's glory' — supposedly a reference to the bad weather that often accompanied the game. Later this was prefixed with 'Kick away both Whig and Tory', though the significance of this is lost. The half dozen or so characters in the procession were in fancy dress, with their faces daubed with soot and red ochre. A drummer accompanied whistle players, and sometimes a fiddler, who attempted to render the traditional 'football tune'. All witnesses agree, however, that the noise they made could scarcely be called music. There was always a man dressed as a woman, who exchanged banter with the onlookers. Most important of all, though, at least one of the group carried a collecting box for contributions. In theory the money went to pay for any damage to the windows and paintwork of the town centre shops that might result from the game: in practice, though, most was spent on drink in the pubs afterwards.

Soon after midday the shops were closed and shuttered, and the fragile street lamps covered with sacking. After barricading their premises, the shop assistants had the rest of the day as a holiday, and many would join the crowd that began to assemble to see the fun. As the clock struck two, the first ball was kicked off from the top of Church Passage, a privilege claimed by the Town Crier, John Sandford, from the 1860s until his death in 1895. This first ball was the Boy's Ball, and comparatively few youngsters joined in at first. They observed the tradition that the Eastenders played the Westenders, the church passage marking the boundary, and each side tried to keep the ball in their own territory. After an hour, a second ball was sent off, but the really important one was the large, gilded ball that started at 5 o'clock. By this time the crowd of players had usually grown to several hundred men, young and not so young. The play was very rough but generally good humoured. If the ball was carried into a pub, it was the tradition to take a break for a quick drink before the ball was thrown back into play from an upper window. An early feature of the game used to be splashing through the blood and other filth that had flowed out from the slaughterhouse in West Street, and also violent duckings in the brook: these, wisely, had been given up by the 1870s. The play grew more and more agressive and tense as 6 o'clock approached, for whichever side held the ball in their territory when the church clock struck was the winner for the year. The West usually triumphed, simply because there were more people living in the western part of the town. The Eastenders are recorded as having won only seven times, and in 1866 this was only because they were reinforced by navvies building the London & Brighton Railway nearby.

After 6 o'clock the town rapidly returned to normal. Many of the footballers held a dinner at the Sun, their headquarters, and that part of the collection not claimed for damages was convivially spent. As a rival attraction to the demon drink, the Church of England Temperance Society gave a free tea party after the game in the years around 1890.

A boisterous and comparatively harmless sport, one might think, but opinion was turning against it. The first move to end it, in the 1850s, was unsuccessful, as the magistrate noted that respectable tradesmen were playing. By the 1890s, however, the respectable classes had largely withdrawn, and a group of High Street tradesmen made an official complaint about the obstruction of the highway and their loss of business. The local authority, the Dorking Urban District Council, was, perhaps surprisingly, strongly in favour of the game continuing — and indeed one of the councillors was an active player of the game. The Surrey County Council overruled them, however, and in 1897 large numbers of police broke up the game. The old custom died hard, and attempts were made to keep it alive for nearly ten years. Eventually though, arrests and fines made it impossible for this to continue and street football was seen no more. The old cross-frame that carried the balls in procession is now in Dorking Museum — the last memorial to Shrove Tuesday football in Surrey.

The Foolish Villages

There is a widespread human tendency, a regrettable one perhaps, to poke fun at a particular group of people: a nation, a region, or merely the inhabitants of a certain village. The most famous example is Gotham in Nottinghamshire. The 'Wise Men of Gotham' were apparently capable of any stupidity or comic misunderstanding. However, exactly the same stories are told all over the country, and each area seems to have chosen a local target as the butt of these jokes. In west Surrey there was the saying 'You don't have to go to Pirbright to find a fool.'

Legend relates how the people of Pirbright considered that their church was too low and mean for a village of such importance. A meeting was held to consider means of raising the height of the church. Many proposals were made and rejected until someone suggested manure. This was a splendid method of making things grow and it was agreed to manure the church. All the dung in the village was collected and dumped against the church walls. That night the rain poured down — and washed down the manure piled against the walls. It left stains behind, though, and when the villagers gathered in the morning they agreed that the church had risen several inches during the night. There was nothing like dung!

Rain had an affinity for Pirbright, it would seem. The inhabitants were so dim-witted that they could only tell it was raining by looking at the surface of ponds. If it did come on to rain, moreover, their first concern was to drive the fish under the bridges to keep them dry. Perhaps the most famous pond story of all is also told of the Pirbrighters. Seeing the full moon reflected in the water, they tried to fish it out with rakes. This tale is told of many places in England, but often one comes across those who proudly call themselves 'Moonrakers' under the impression that their village alone has this distinction. Foolish indeed.

Why Pirbright should have acquired this reputation is hard to say. Possibly the fact that it was an isolated hamlet among some of the least fertile heathland in England led it to be considered backward. Indeed a stranger was such a rare sight there in the early 1800s that the villagers would link hands and dance round him in a circle. This was known as 'Dancing the Hog', and it may have been a way of extracting a tip from the new arrival.

Chobham, too, is a heathland village with poor soil. 'Two pairs of anything would make a Chobham orchard' was a local proverb. 'Chobhamners', as they were called, were supposed to have webbed feet, though it is a dry rather than marshy area. They were also said to put their pigs on the wall to watch military bands go by. There must have been many of these — bands, that is, not pigs — when Queen Victoria reviewed the army on Chobham Common in 1853. This was supposed to be the origin of another saying, that 'Chobham is where the treacle mines are'. In theory, barrels of treacle surplus to the army's requirements were buried when the camps broke up. If we accept that the War Department was so reckless with its supplies, we might be convinced by this explanation — were it not for the fact that dozens of treacle-well villages are scattered all over the country — almost as many as 'moonraker' villages.

A reputation for foolishness is easily acquired and hard to shake off. Before the last war, a party of Chobhamners out carol singing one night came across a house and struck up a carol. No matter how long they sang, however, no light appeared and nobody came to the door. At length a direct approach was decided upon, a torch was switched on to light the way — and revealed that the darkened house was nothing but a haystack. You may be sure that this incident was quoted as further proof of the eccentricities of Chobham.

Ripley, too, found it all too easy to become considered a village of fools, by the the people of Old Woking, if nobody else. In the early years of the present century a blacksmith cast a horse to shoe it — that is, tied its hooves and laid it down on the grass of the village green. However, while the smith was shoeing all four feet, the poor horse died of heart failure. The smith did not notice this, and when he had finished, he unhobbled the horse and flapped his apron to make it rise to its feet. Nothing happened, and the apron was flapped more and more vigorously until the truth dawned on the unfortunate man. For years afterwards it was a standing joke with the people of Woking to call Ripley 'the place where they shoe dead horses', and every time they met a Ripley man they would flap an imaginary apron at him. The reputation was quickly established. At about the same time a man trimming trees on an estate west of Byfleet sawed off the branch on which he was sitting and fell into the Basingstoke Canal. When a girl from Old Woking heard of this she merely commented 'I expect that was a Ripley man.' Unfortunately, it was.

These tales, it goes without saying, are quite unfair and often the teller will insist that, whatever the reputation for folly in the past, the current inhabitants of the village in question are as sensible as you and I. Not, when you think about it, much of a reassurance.

The Anchoress
of Shere

S t. James, Shere, is one of the most pleasant churches in Surrey,
its shingled spire rising high above the village that nestles in
the valley between the North Downs and the sand ridge. Shere is
a picturesque spot, and one that attracts many visitors — rather
too many, perhaps, in the opinion of some of the residents. In
the 14th century, however, this tranquil, rural village was the
scene of a minor ecclesiastical crisis and a major personal tragedy
— that of Christine, the Anchoress of Shere.

Anchorites and anchoresses were people who decided to give
up life in the wicked world and literally 'anchor' themselves to
the church. This usually took the form of being walled up in a
small cell attached to an existing church. There would be an iron-
barred window through which food would be delivered to them,
and a small opening through the wall into the church through
which they could take part in the services and receive the com-
munion. But there would be no door. It was intended that the
anchorite would stay in that tiny cell until death released the soul
to enjoy its eternal reward. In the Middle Ages people of all kinds
became anchorites; young and old, priests and laymen, and many
women. Some wealthy ladies even arranged for their serving
maids to be shut in with them, and some 'anchorages' were, if not
luxurious, at least as comfortable as any other mediaeval home.

In June 1329 Christine, the daughter of William the carpenter
of Shere, felt the call to become an anchoress. As the regulations
demanded, she wrote (or more probably had written for her) a
letter to John Stratford, the Bishop of Winchester, in whose dio-
cese Shere then lay. She asked for permission to be 'enclosed' at
St. James' church, so that she might more easily live a pious life

37

in the service of God, away from the pleasures and distractions of the outside world. The bishop was cautious at first. He had known cases before where religious fervour had led people into commitments which they afterwards regretted, and so he ordered a formal enquiry. The rector and parishioners of Shere must summon Christine to a sworn examination at the church. Anyone who felt they could contribute to the enquiry was to question her individually and satisfy themselves that she was sincere, and that her faith was strong enough to carry out the binding vows she would have to take. They had to ensure that she was chaste, and not engaged to any man, and finally the parson and the villagers must themselves be agreeable to her request.

The enquiry was duly held, and satisfactory answers returned to the bishop. Christine was determined to go ahead, the rector Matthew Redeman and his flock approved, and so the bishop's licence was granted. The stone cell was built on the north side of the chancel of St. James'. There were two openings into the church; one a narrow, angled slot that would allow the anchoress to watch the solemn ritual of the mass at the high altar, and a small hole with a quatrefoil surround through which she would receive the sacrament. The ceremony of enclosure would have been impressive. The young woman would have had to take a vow never to leave the narrow confines of her chosen anchorage, and as she entered it through the small gap left by the stonemason, parts from the burial service were read. She was, in the eyes of the church, dead — dead to the sinful, earthly world but alive to the eternal salvation of Heaven. As the last stones were mortared into place, she must have felt that this was the supreme moment of her life.

Sadly, though, the bishop's initial reservations were justified. Christine endured her confinement for two or three years, but eventually she could bear it no longer. Somehow, perhaps on her own, or perhaps with outside help, she broke out of her cell and once more walked in the open air. The pleasures of freedom, however, were not to last long. We will never know whether she repented of her vow-breaking herself, or whether repentance was forced on her by her family and neighbours, appalled at the disgrace brought on their village. In any event, she came, or was sent, to the bishop in October 1332, bearing a letter in which she beseeched the bishop and the Pope to forgive her weakness and fall from grace. The bishop decided to give her another chance. She had to allow herself to be re-enclosed within four months or face excommunication from the Christian church. If during her brief period of freedom she was tempted by the Devil and sinned, then the bishop hinted darkly to the Dean of Guildford that she might even be liable to punishment of death. The dean was to see her safely walled up once more, and after a period of good behaviour had proved she was going to live up to her vows, some suitably harsh penance must be imposed on her for the dreadful sin of breaking them.

It is not certain that Christine was in fact re-enclosed — but in all probability she was. The fear of excommunication and certain damnation to hell would have been unbearable to a religious person. Compared with that, life long imprisonment was almost to be welcomed. We cannot tell how long she stayed in her cell before death set her free, nor what thoughts passed through her mind as she stared through the iron grating that separated her forever from the sunshine, the grass, and the trees that grew beside the shallow-flowing Tillingbourne. All that is left to remind us of her are the slot and the quatrefoil openings in the chancel wall of St. James' church, now gazing blankly out from where was once the little cell that was the whole world of Christine, the carpenter's daughter.

Timber-Framed Houses

Surrey is blessed with a large number of fine timber-framed houses. While there is little suitable building stone, the oak woodland that used to cover much of the county provided the ideal building material, so sturdy and durable that most of the houses built three or four centuries ago are still standing and still occupied as homes. The majority, that is, in rural areas: in towns many have been demolished as pressure on town centres led to re-development. A surprising number still survive, however, 'up-dated' by adding a facade in Georgian times when timber-framing was thought old-fashioned and uncouth.

Late mediaeval and early Tudor houses had a standard plan, with very little variation one from another. At the centre was a large hall, open right up to the very apex of the roof. An open fire burnt in the middle of the hall, the smoke rising up to the rafters and percolating out through vents or louvres. Much of the life of the house went on in the hall; the master and servants eating together, perhaps the menservants and young farm-workers actually sleeping round the fire. The master and his family would have two private rooms at the 'upper' end of the hall, a 'parlour' on the ground floor and a 'solar' above. At the 'lower' end was the cross-passage that ran from the front door straight to the back and beyond the passage two doors that led to the buttery (where drink was kept) and the pantry (where food was stored). Perhaps the maidservants would sleep in the room above the pantry and the buttery.

These, of course, would have been the homes of farmers rather than farm labourers. The married workers would have lived in more modest dwellings which usually retained some features of the standard plan. In town centres, too, the plan needed modification. Pressure of space demanded that the end rather than the long side must front the street. A passage had therefore to run the length of the house, past the shop or craftman's workshop that often occupied the ground floor frontage. A good example survives in Milkhouse Gate, a narrow alley leading off Guildford's High Street. It has also been suggested that the need for more space resulted in the upper floors being 'jettied', projecting a foot or more beyond the wall below. However, since this feature is found in country farmhouses with all the space they need, it may simply have been a fashion.

Fashion is ever-changing in all aspects of life, and in Tudor times there grew a desire for greater privacy. Rather than dining in the hall, the master began eating separately with his family in the parlour. To provide more individual rooms, attempts were made to board over the open hall at first floor level. This naturally left the problem of how the smoke from the fire was to escape. It was not until bricks became widely available in the mid 1500s that chimneys became a practical solution. The hall gradually declined in status and in modern houses it is merely the small lobby inside the front door.

The bricks that built the chimneys were, within a hundred years, to build the walls of houses as well. The great oak forests had been felled and suitable timber was getting rarer and more costly. Still, the fine old timber-framed houses remain and have become highly esteemed properties, so much so that many later imitations have been built. Some are quite convincing and only betray their lack of authenticity by deviating from the genuine plan. Others merely copy the style in the clumsiest of ways, as in the rows of semi-detached suburban houses with planks nailed to the brickwork in imitation of oak beams.

It has to be said, on the other hand, that the pride the householder takes in his genuine timber-framed house is not always an educated pride. A body of modern folklore has grown up which abounds in misconceptions. Perhaps the most famous old chestnut is that the house is built of old ships' timbers. 'You can see where the original joints were,' cries the owner 'they must have brought the timbers up from the coast' (or something to that effect). Certainly these timbers show mortices and scarfs from earlier joints — but in every case they are from buildings, not ships. Ships' timbers are quite unsuitable for house-building but the tale is told time and time again.

Another common misapprehension is that the small cupboard or chamber set into the old, wide chimney was a priest hole. These in truth were nothing more nor less than bacon lofts, where sides of bacon were hung to be smoked. It is quite impossible, though, to understand why breweries, when doing up old pubs, should imagine that the Tudor carpenter was a wild maniac, hacking the timbers about with an axe to leave a rough, mottled surface. All about us are hundreds of well-preserved examples of the craftsman's work, finely adzed beams as smooth as if they had been planed. The breweries know better, however, and our pubs are full of chopped and battered beams.

Perhaps worse, though, is the passion for black and white. There is a deep-seated mental image that all cottages should have black beams with white infilling. Indeed, in the west Midlands and elsewhere, this was the traditional style. In Surrey, however, we limewashed the whole surface, or left the oak its natural, silvery colour. The desire for a black and white cottage has even led some owners to strip the traditional tile-hanging from their upper walls and dutifully paint black the spindly timbers beneath that were never intended to be exposed. Still, despite the indignities that some suffer, the fine old timber-framed houses of Surrey will last for centuries yet — certainly long after most of the buildings which are put up today have fallen down.

William Cobbett

William Cobbett was born at the Jolly Farmer, Farnham in 1762. His father was not only the landlord, but a farmer himself, and his young son was put to work on the land as soon as he was able. After a day spent keeping birds off the newly-seeded ground he had to make his way home over gates and stiles he was hardly big enough to clamber over. He loved the outdoor life of the country, and while his father taught him elementary reading and writing in the evenings, Cobbett later considered that the rough-and-tumble play with his boyhood friends was a better education than any public school or university could have given him.

He rapidly developed the independence and sense of justice that were later to shape his career. This is illustrated by a tale from when he was about eight. He had been following the harriers to the kill on Seale Common, and the boy darted into the pack of hounds to seize the hare. A huntsman named Bradley lashed the boy with his whip, which the young William resented as unjust. Rather than brooding on this, he planned his revenge. The next time the harriers were out, William tied a red herring on a string and trailed it about over Seale Common — and eventually into a swamp. Sure enough the hounds followed the false scent and led the frustrated and cursing huntsmen aimlessly about before taking them thigh-deep into the mud and slime. All the while the boy was looking on with ill-concealed satisfaction.

He spent nineteen happy years in Farnham, until the urge to travel spurred him on. A visit to see the fleet at Portsmouth prompted him to go and enlist for a sailor, but he was turned down. Returning home, he was taken by a sudden impulse and caught the coach to London, where a job as a clerk was found for him. This tedious desk-bound life was quite the opposite of the adventure he longed for, and at length he gave it up and joined

43

the Marines. At least he thought he had joined the Marines. In fact he had been enlisted into an infantry regiment bound overseas to America. He served there for eight years, and his evident keenness and above-average intelligence brought him rapid promotion to sergeant-major. Encouraged by his colonel, Cobbett spent a great deal of his time improving his written English. This was to stand him in good stead in his later career.

His sense of natural justice, however, was shocked by the widespread corruption that pervaded the army, and when he returned to England in 1792 he tried to raise the matter with the authorities. By this time he had left the army and married a pretty and hard-working girl he had met in America. The government, riddled with corruption itself, did not take kindly to Cobbett's accusations and in reply a charge of treason was trumped up against him. He fled to France, but the outbreak of the Revolutionary 'Terror' sent him on to America again. There he became involved in politics, and adopted the pen-name 'Peter Porcupine' in his attacks on the Democrats and the French Revolutionaries. His spirited defence of England and the King earned him friends in the British government — but powerful enemies in America.

Another trumped-up law case ruined him, and he had to return to England.

He had left eight years before with the government threatening him with a treason charge; now he returned to a hero's welcome and government approval. He started up a newspaper, *The Porcupine* in which he set out his own rather prickly and individual brand of Toryism. Despite the approval of Prime Minister Pitt and his government, however, the paper failed. Moreover, Cobbett was beginning to realise the vast scale of the corruption that pervaded the highest places in the land, and the bad effect this had on the lives of working people. He began another paper, his *Political Register,* which attacked government misconduct. Pitt and his ministers turned on their former ally, and yet another unfair charge led to Cobbett being imprisoned for two years. The *Register* continued to be printed, nevertheless, and in the depression that followed the Napoleonic Wars he called for wide-reaching political and social reforms. The government again moved against him and once more he went into self-imposed exile in America in 1817. On his return two years later he was forced into bankruptcy but the *Register* continued nonetheless.

Cobbett began now to pour out the flood of writing that was to establish him as a major political and literary figure. In particular his *Rural Rides* began to appear as a series from 1821. He travelled the country, describing the state of the agriculture he saw and the lot of the working people he met. Perceptively and convincingly he argued the case for reform. He had a tendency to be rather lavish with his praise for the Surrey countryside, for example describing Farnham as 'the neatest (spot) in England, and, I believe, in the whole world', Guildford as 'the most agreeable and most happy-looking (town) that I ever saw in my life' and considered there to be 'very few prettier rides in England' than the road from Buckland through Dorking to Albury. The oak tree on Tilford green was 'the finest thing I ever saw in my life', and so on. This hyperbole underlines the genuine enthusiasm he had for the countryside, although he was not uncritical at times. The wide, infertile wastes of heathland offended his farmer's eye, and the beautiful Tillingbourne valley at Chilworth was perverted, in his opinion, by 'two of the most damnable inventions that ever sprang from the minds of men under the influence of the devil: namely, the making of gunpowder and of bank-notes!'

Poverty and unemployment led to riots in 1830, which were blamed on Cobbett's social agitation. His trial the following year cleared him, though, and by implication blamed the government. Reform was now irresistible, and Cobbett took his seat as M.P. for Oldham in the reformed Parliament of 1832. He was to be disappointed, however, by its failure to improve the lot of the working man. He died at his farm at Wyke, near Ash, in 1835 and is buried in his family tomb in Farnham churchyard.

He is difficult to place in terms of modern politics. He was a fiercely independent conservative, defending the king and the constitution, and at the same time he had a deep respect and concern for the working man, and the farm labourer in particular. His birthplace, the Jolly Farmer, has now been renamed the William Cobbett, a fitting tribute to the beer-loving politician whose vigorous and compassionate opinions were heard many miles beyond the borders of his native Surrey.

The Surrey Puma

William Cobbett recalled an incident which must have occurred in about 1770. There was a hollow elm tree near Waverley Abbey 'into which I, when a little boy, once saw a cat go, that was as big as a middle-sized spaniel dog, for which relating I got a great scolding, for standing to which I, at last, got a beating, but stand to which I did. I have since many times repeated it, and would take my oath on it to this day. When in New Brunswick I saw the great wild grey cat, which is there called a Lucifee, and it seemed to me to be just such a cat as I had seen at Waverley.' As well as illustrating the young radical's steadfast determination to stick to what he thought was the truth, this is also the first, and for two hundred years the only, account of what has become known as the 'Surrey Puma'. Strictly speaking, it has been sighted as much in Hampshire as Surrey, and from conflicting descriptions may be anything from a puma to a lynx, a panther, or a lion cub . . . or none of them. Still, the name has stuck to a creature that has often been seen, sometimes photographed, but never, ever caught.

The sightings seem to have begun around 1960 in the area west of Farnham, and soon reports of strange, large cats were coming in from all over west Surrey. From 1962 to 1964, for example, the Godalming police were receiving reports at an average rate of one every two days. The elusive animal leapt to national prominence, though, in September 1964. A man was picking blackberries in his lunch hour near the water tower on Munstead Heath. Suddenly he disturbed a creature in the bushes, which he later described as being three feet high, five feet long, and with a cat's face and long tail. It was golden brown in colour, with a dark stripe down the back. It snarled and spat at the blackberry-picker, who did not stay to observe it more closely. Indeed, he left rather hurriedly. Some days later a long trail of huge paw-prints was discovered at Stilemans nearby. They were over five inches wide, and the tracks ended at a high chain-link fence, over which the animal must have jumped. Later the same month a deer and a heifer were reported as having been attacked by a creature inflicting terrible scratches, and a driver at Dunsfold claimed to have seen a puma run across the road in front of him. The attention of the public was fully aroused and Dr Maurice Burton of Albury, a distinguished naturalist, was called in. He was shown plaster casts of the Munstead paw-prints, which had already been identified by London Zoo — perhaps rather hastily — as puma. Not so, said Dr Burton, pointing out the dog-like grouping of the toes. But, it was protested, no claw marks were visible: cats can withdraw their claws, dogs cannot. However, Dr Burton's enquiries revealed that pedigree bloodhound's claws are positioned high above the toe-pads and may not show in a shallow print. Subsequent checks showed that these claw marks were indeed visible in some of the Munstead prints. Furthermore, bloodhound paws as wide as 5¼ inches were not impossible.

This pooh-poohing of the puma did not go down well with those who were rather taken with the idea of a dangerous wild animal on the loose in the heart of 'civilised' Surrey. The police even went so far as to warn the public away from the heathland between Peaslake and Albury where the cat was supposed to be spending the winter — despite the fact that no attacks on humans had been reported. In 1966 a series of sightings in the Worplesdon, Hog's Back and Seale areas were also referred to Dr Burton, who was able to explain them as dogs, foxes, and other normal animals. A police inspector retorted that he was familiar with such creatures and what he and his men had seen was a puma. (It may be recalled, incidentally, that the Surrey constabulary has also reported flying saucers at Ash.) Sightings continued in west Surrey and no doubt many a fox's raid on a chicken-run was blamed on the Puma. A novelist, Andrew Sinclair, used the idea for a fictional account of 'The Surrey Cat', in which a panther terrorises Wanborough before being killed.

There seems to have been a lull in puma sightings until January 1970, when a house-wife walking on Ash Ranges heard a terrifying screeching, followed by the appearance of a brown cat as large as a labrador. The Surrey Puma once more reared its feline head in its old hunting grounds and further reports came in; from Bagshot in 1972, for example, and Bramley the following year.

Another three or four year gap was ended in 1977, when a motorist saw an animal the size of a retriever, but loping like a cat, in Mid Street, South Nutfield. Farm workers saw a similar creature at Send in 1979 and a couple walking with their dog at Pockford near Chiddingfold came across a dark honey-coloured animal with a pale belly in 1980, shortly after another sighting at East Horsley. Yet another report came from Holmbury St. Mary in 1981. Indeed, I have to admit that I saw the puma myself shortly after. Driving one night between Grafham and Bramley, I saw a pair of glowing green eyes reflected in the headlights. A large dun-coloured creature was trotting along the verge, with a long, drooping tail: a large cat, most assuredly. Having driven past, I turned the car and went back, convinced I had seen the Surrey Puma and wishing to get a closer look. What I found was a rather emaciated mongrel dog, with a lot of the Great Dane about him. Had I not driven back, one more sighting of the Surrey Puma would have been reported.

Surrey is not unique in this phenomenon. Large cat-like creatures have been rumoured to be roaming many parts of the country — the 'Beast of Exmoor' causing a national stir in 1983, in particular. All have one thing in common, however. No specimen is ever caught, alive or dead. Like the Loch Ness monster, we have only eye witness accounts and inconclusive photographs. Expert naturalists are generally sceptical, but the public is enthusiastic. This being so, we can expect to hear more of the Surrey Puma.

The Earl of Holland's Rising

In the spring of 1648 there was great discontent in Surrey. The Civil War fought to protect individual liberty against the tyranny of the king was over. Charles I was a prisoner on the Isle of Wight and Oliver Cromwell was busy establishing himself as the political leader of the army, laying the groundwork for a military dictatorship. The people of Surrey had paid heavily in cash and in kind to support the Parliamentarian armies, in the hope that peace would leave them better off than before. It did not. The fighting was over, but the army refused to disband and had already quarrelled with its erstwhile masters in Parliament. Meanwhile, the soldiers in Surrey were at 'free quarter', living in the civilians' houses and eating their food without paying a penny — and behaving in a menacing fashion if any protests were offered. In truth, the officers had little control over their men, and the people of Surrey had become heartily fed up with them.

Many desired a return to the old and familiar system of government under the King. The crushing taxation, the high prices, the impositions on their freedom were all worse than they had been under Charles I. A compromise between him and Parliament seemed the only solution. In a thoroughly constitutional way, therefore, a petition was organised throughout the county. Meetings were held at Leatherhead, Dorking, and Guildford, and some 5,000 signatures collected, demanding the return of the King and the disbanding of the army. On 16th May about a thousand people escorted the Surrey Petition to the House of Commons. For some reason an ugly scuffle broke out with the soldiers on guard and in the ensuing riot several people were killed. The rest returned to their homes angry and bitter.

It would seem that the county of Surrey was ripe for rebellion against Parliament; so at least was the opinion of some ardent Royalists. The leaders of this conspiracy did not inspire confidence, though. The Earl of Holland had changed sides twice in the war, and the Earl of Peterborough and the Duke of Buckingham were young and without experience. They were not Surrey men, and their amateurish plotting in London was soon well known to Parliament's spies. The government issued instructions to secure castles in Surrey against possible insurgents and Sir Richard Onslow, who had controlled Surrey for Parliament in the Civil War, was cautioned to be on his guard. Onslow seems to have been ambiguous in his loyalty now, and arranged matters so that he took no active part in what was to follow.

Holland moved neither swiftly nor in co-operation with Royalists in neighbouring counties. On the 5th July, however, he was ready and rode across the Thames into Kingston at the head of 500 horsemen. After a few hours' stay he marched on over Banstead Downs to Reigate, where he occupied the town. It is clear that he had no real objective in mind, and thought that all that was necessary to provoke an uprising was to appear in arms and the country people would flock to join him. Like many rebels before and since, he was at a loss what to do when they didn't.

A few recruits did appear, in fact, but nobody had considered bringing spare arms and horses for them. Confusion and indecision reigned — and time began to run out for the small force in Reigate. Parliament had moved fast when Holland showed his hand, and troops from Hounslow, Horsham, and Kent converged on him. The first he knew of their arrival was the appearance of their advance guard on the Downs above Redhill, forcing his own scouts to fall back into Reigate. Mustering his men, Holland marched out of the town to Dorking, where they spent the night. At dawn, however, he was informed that Reigate was still unoccupied by the enemy and so he decided to march back again. It is obvious that nobody among the Royalists had any notion as to the correct way to conduct a campaign. No advance or flank guards were sent out, and the whole column fell into disarray when a party of unidentified riders came to meet them. Chaos reigned as those in front tried to ride back through those behind, and many ran into the woods beside the road. The strangers turned out to be sympathisers who warned Holland that the Roundheads were indeed in Reigate.

Hearing this, Holland turned north and headed back towards Kingston — but fate was at his heels. The Parliamentarian advance guard under Sir Michael Livesey caught up with his stragglers not far from Nonsuch Palace, outside Ewell. In order to allow his foot soldiers to reach Kingston, Holland drew up his horsemen on Kingston Common, not far from where Surbiton Station now stands. Livesey's own cavalry lined up opposite them and waited. This suited Livesey well, as it gave time for the rest of his soldiers to catch up. There was some sporadic firing and a few hot-blooded individuals advanced from the opposing ranks to offer single combat, but it was not until dusk that Livesey was ready. He charged Holland, and Holland charged him. The struggle seemed equal until a second wave of Paliamentarians under Major Gibbons crashed into the Royalist ranks. Musket fire poured into their flanks from the hedgerows and field guns may even have been used — an iron roundshot has been found near the spot in recent years. Holland's men broke and fled, and did not draw rein until they reached Kingston. The handsome Lord Francis Villiers dismounted, and held off a group of enemy swordsmen with his back to a tree until one crept round behind and killed him.

Livesey waited until daylight before entering Kingston, but Holland's men had all slipped away in the night. The Earl himself was taken prisoner two days later, having done little to further the King's cause. Holland was tried and condemned to death the following year, not for his rebellion, but for deserting the godly cause of Parliament. His appeal for a reprieve was turned down by 31 votes to 30 and he was beheaded on 9th March 1649. He had failed to appreciate that when Parliament had ended 'free quarter' for their soldiers at the end of May, the major cause of discontent had been removed. The people of Surrey had seen all they wanted of soldiers, whether Royalist or Parliamentarian, and they had no desire to revive the flames of civil war.

The Surrey Iron Railway

At the end of the eighteenth century, Britain was hard pressed in the war against France. Her survival depended largely on her sea trade, but ships sailing through the straits of Dover to enter the Thames were frequently attacked by privateers from the French coast nearby. To avoid this hazard, a scheme was proposed for a canal and railway linking London and Portsmouth, where ships could unload in comparative safety. At first a canal from Wandsworth to Croydon was suggested. However, it was discovered that this would take too much water away from the River Wandle, where it was needed to turn the wheels of the dozens of mills along its banks. The Wandle valley was at that time one of the most densely industrialised parts of England. So a horse-drawn railway was decided upon and in 1801 the Surrey Iron Railway Company was formed.

William Jessop was appointed as the engineer. He had more experience of dock and canal building, but had used and developed railways as part of some of the projects he had undertaken. He began work on the nine mile line from the Thames at Wandsworth through Merton and Mitcham to Croydon. The rails were of cast iron, L-shape in section with a high inner flange, and these were laid on stone blocks rather than wooden sleepers. The flanges kept the waggons on the rails and meant that the wheels could have a flat rim, unlike modern railway wheels. The Company was quick to point out the advantage of this: the railway waggons could be taken off the rails and hauled to their final destination on ordinary roads without having to unload and re-load. In the event this doesn't seem to have been done very often, and the fact that the pairs of wheels had to be a standard distance

apart — 4½ feet — meant that most ordinary road waggons weren't able to take to the rails themselves. The railway waggons were built of wood, with iron wheels — and naturally were drawn by horses. Steam engines were very much in the experimental stage, and horses were still the most practical form of power. There was one important difference, though, between the Surrey Iron Railway and its predecessors. Whereas previously railways were usually privately owned by coal mines and connected them to canals, the S.I.R. was open to anyone with any goods to carry. The Company simply owned the track, and the waggons and horses were provided by anyone who wished to use it. They were charged a toll per mile, which varied with the goods carried. So when the Surrey Iron Railway opened on 26th July 1803 it was the first public railway in the world.

A branch to Carshalton was opened in the following year, by which time a separate company had been set up; the Croydon, Merstham, and Godstone Iron Railway. The C.M. & G.R. intended to extend the line to Reigate and eventually to Portsmouth. Unfortunately the going was not as easy as the route of the S.I.R. In order to avoid steep gradients which the horses would find difficult, cuttings, embankments, and bridges were needed. These were expensive and slow to build, and the C.M. & G.R. had only reached as far as the quarries at Merstham before Nelson's victory at Trafalgar reduced the threat to British shipping and so reduced the pressure for an overland route to the south coast.

The line from Merstham to Croydon was opened in July 1805 with the winning of a remarkable wager. A single horse was challenged to pull twelve waggons loaded with stone the length of the six-mile track. The waggons were loaded and coupled up, and a horse chosen at random and harnessed to the train. Immediately the advantages of smooth iron rails over rough, rutted roads become obvious. The horse easily started the train moving and pulled it all the way to Croydon at an average speed not much under 4 miles per hour (although the usual working speed was more like 2½ m.p.h.). Each waggon carried over three tons of stone, so the total weight pulled was over 36 tons. After the destination had been reached and the wager won, four more loaded waggons were hitched on, and fifty of the workmen who had built the line clambered aboard, making a total weight for the train of over 55 tons. The horse pulled this weight also, with little difficulty.

Despite this demonstration of efficiency, the Croydon, Merstham, and Godstone Railway was never really a financial success. The steam locomotive was rapidly being developed, and it was not long before it outstripped the horse as the best way of pulling waggons on rails. It was no coincidence that when the company was sold up in 1838 it was bought by the London and Brighton Railway, which needed the Hooley to Merstham stretch as part of their intended steam railway to the coast.

The Surrey Iron Railway lasted a little longer, and was a little more successful than the C.M. & G.R., carrying raw materials and finished products for the industries along the Wandle. Travelling only at a walking pace, however, it was not really suitable for passengers and by the 1840s it was clear that the days of the horse-drawn railway were over. The S.I.R. was abandoned in 1846 and dismantled two years later. The course of the S.I.R. and the C.M. & G.R. can still be traced, and some of the rails and stone

blocks have been preserved. A section of track has been recon-
structed in a garden on Merstham High Street and blocks, rails
and an iron waggon wheel are on display at Guildford Museum.
Little else remains, though, as a reminder of the first public railway in the world.

Garland Day

⮌⮎

In 1891 the rector of Ockley lamented that 'an old custom seems to be dying out, that of children bringing round garlands of flowers on May-day. It may be well for it to do so if ragged bunches of flowers tied to the end of a stick are made the only excuse for asking a penny. But time was when the flowers were arranged with a certain amount of art and beauty. Three or four hoops covered lightly with green leaves and flowers, and linked together as a chain, or crossed and interlaced together in the shape of a globe, or a wreath or festoon hanging gracefully. These, if daintily made, were a pleasure to see, and a penny was readily forthcoming as a tribute of welcome to the evidences of a brighter and pleasanter time of the year.'

May garlands such as the rector describes were carried in many parts of the country during the last century, and the custom is still preserved in some places. As with any other tradition, however, we must not presume that this had been done 'from time immemorial'. Customs are born, grow, and die with surprising speed, and there is nothing to suggest that children carried May garlands in Surrey until the early 1800s. The custom flourished in the middle of the century, but by the 1890s it was clearly on the decline. This decline can, in fact, be plotted quite accurately from school log-books, which meticulously kept records of truancy. After all, the teacher's pay was affected by attendances. For example, at the Boys' National School at Dorking on 1st May 1864 there was 'a small attendance of boys owing to its being Garland day.' References to truancy continue throughout the century, rapidly falling off until it is last mentioned in 1905. The same pattern can be seen in other Surrey schools and the custom barely managed to stagger over the threshold of the 20th century before collapsing. The end was hastened by the artificial May revels organised by the schools themselves. These had their roots in John Ruskin's invention of a May Queen ceremony at the Whitelands Teachers' Training College in 1888. Amongst other ideas, he introduced the ribbon-plaiting Maypole dance which he had come across as part of the repertoire of professional dancing-masters and imagined that it was the Old English Maypole dance. Ruskin's May Day was enthusiastically adopted by primary school teachers, who introduced it into their schools under the well-meaning impression that they were helping to revive 'Merry England.' In 1904, 'May Day sports' were officially organised at the Girls' School at Dorking at the same time as the unofficially organised garland carrying ceased at the Boys' School.

The garlands themselves are well described by the rector of Ockley and, as he notes, the elaborate, hooped variety degenerated into simply a stick with flowers tied to it by the end of the century. It is not surprising, therefore, that these were sometimes referred to as 'maypoles' — the tall, permanent maypoles that once stood on many village greens in Surrey had all disappeared by the 1850s (except for the one at Wood Street). Still, it can be rather confusing to see an entry such as 'Children absent maypoling' without being aware that this was another name for garland-carrying.

The garlands were carried from door to door, the children chanting a rhyme to each person they visited. The usual rhyme in Surrey went

> The First of May is Garland Day
> So please remember the garland.
> We only come here but once a year,
> So please remember the garland.

There were many variations, though — a particularly interesting one was remembered by a lady born at Oatlands near Weybridge in 1893:

> Maypole garland, the first of May is Maypole Day.
> The second of May is chimney sweep, the dancing day.
> We only come here but once a year,
> Please remember the maypole.
> A bunch of flowers I've brought you
> And at your door I stand.
> It's a lovely time and a lovely day
> And we come from the Lord's right hand.

May Day was the chimney-sweeping boy's holiday, and they would dance through the streets of the towns, often accompanied by a man in a wicker framework completely covered in leaves — 'Jack-in-the-Green'. This custom died out soon after sweep's boys were banned in 1864. The last four lines are a fragment of a well-known May carol. Not all rhymes were as elaborate as that from Oatlands, however. At Kingston and Hambledon the message was more direct.

> The first of May is Garland Day,
> Give me a penny and I'll go away.

You may be sure that the wealthier residents were not omitted from the circuit of visits. A penny was the expected reward at each stop, although one lady at Limpsfield in the middle of the last century regularly gave a silver fourpence. Buns and cakes were also forthcoming, and Mr Horn, a Guildford draper, gave out pictorial pocket handkerchiefs in the 1870s. The money collected was usually divided among the children in the group, perhaps being the largest sum of money they received the whole year round. In early Victorian Dorking, furthermore, they could sell the garlands to a grocer who paid a penny for each, and at the end of the day as many as fifty could be seen hanging outside his shop.

But as we have seen, Garland Day was all but dead by the time of the First World War. A great pity, surely, and would it not be fine to see once more, not the artificial school ceremony of the May Queen and the ribbon-plaiting dance, but the pretty flower-garlands of one of the most attractive customs in our calendar?

Martin Tupper and 'The Silent Pool'

In the middle of the last century there lived in Albury a writer named Martin Tupper, one of the worst poets ever to achieve national and international fame. Indeed, for a time his pompous and ponderous *Proverbial Philosophy* was the most widely read poetry in the English language. This volume of pious platitudes about life and love, expressed in clumsy rhythms and twisted English, appealed to many in the opening years of Queen Victoria's reign. Tupper has been described as 'a poet who did not know what poetry was, who wrote for other people who did not know what poetry was' and the real poets among his contemporaries were not fooled for a moment. Tupper himself had an unshakeable belief in his own brilliance — he was convinced he would be made Poet Laureate — and looked upon the savagery of his critics with puzzled incomprehension rather than resentment. However, the reading public gradually lost interest in Tupper's humourless moralising and he was eventually forgotten, dying in obscurity. Forgotten, that is, except in Surrey, where his name will be remembered here as the author of *Stephan Langton, a Romance of the Silent Pool,* which he wrote in 1858 'to add a new interest in Albury . . . to make our country classic ground.'

The story relates how bad King John, while out hunting near Shere, came across Emma the woodcutter's daughter bathing naked in the Silent Pool. He attempts to have his will of the girl, who prefers to drown rather than submit to his evil advances. The King rides off disappointed, and Emma's brother is also drowned trying to rescue her. The incident comes to the attention of Stephan Langton, born at Friday Street and now a priest with a good reason to detest King John. Before entering the priesthood, Stephan had been in love with a girl who had been kidnapped by the King; she had died of burns sustained in a fire when Stephan

61

had rescued her from the wicked courtiers at Tangley Manor. The public outcry following the tragic drownings enables Langton to begin an undercover campaign against King John. He eventually becomes Archbishop of Canterbury and is able to lead the barons in a united front against the King which leads to the signing of Magna Carta at Runnymede. It turns out, however, that Stephan's former love had not really died of her burns but had lived to become an abbess at St. Catherine's near Guildford. Marriage is now, of course, impossible, but when he dies Stephan Langton leaves instructions for his body to be buried alongside hers at St. Martha's. Their stone coffin-lids may be seen there to this day.

A rattling good yarn, and one in which Tupper was able to indulge his fierce hatred of Catholicism as much as his love for the locality. (Although when he maintains that Stephan Langton was a Protestant forerunner of Martin Luther, one realises just how blinkered his vision was.) Why then should an historical novel, no better and no worse than hundreds of others like it, make such an impact? Simply because Tupper claimed that, far from being a work of fiction, every word of it was true . . . 'or like the truth.' 'It may be depended on for archaeological accuracy in every detail' he assured his readers '. . . rather reality than romance.' This was utterly untrue.

What then, is the truth of the tale? It would be a tedious matter to itemise every false assertion in *Stephan Langton,* but let us consider a few examples that reveal the way Tupper's mind worked. The real Stephan Langton was most probably born at Langton in Lincolnshire, but Tupper wanted him to be a Surrey man — so he had him born at Friday Street (where a pub was later named in his honour). Tupper justifies this by saying that men return to die to the place where they were born, and as Langton died at Slinfold, near Horsham, he must have been born nearby, i.e. Friday Street, about 9 miles away. Whether or not it is true that men do return to die at their birthplace, Tupper was wrong. Langton died not at Slinfold, but at Slindon near Arundel. It is difficult to know whether this was genuine mistake or simply part of the process of making central Surrey 'classic ground.'

The Silent Pool is in reality Sherbourne Pond, a flooded chalkpit almost certainly dug several centuries after Langton's death. There is no historical record of such people as Emma the wood-cutter's daughter or her brother, nor was there ever a nunnery at St. Catherine's. The discovery of the two stone coffin-lids at St. Martha's was the starting point for the story that Tupper went on to invent. To his mind, the crosses on the lids were those of an archbishop and an abbess. Nothing of the sort, in fact; both are perfectly normal mediaeval crosses with no particular associations. One could go on with a long catalogue of similar errors, but all these were unsuspected by the local inhabitants who eagerly read *Stephan Langton* and kept the book in print long after everything else Tupper had written was remaindered. The local reader wanted to believe that every word was true, and there lay the secret of its success.

Scenes from the book were quickly established in their localities. Sherbourne Pond became 'The Silent Pool' and soon began to attract visitors. The 'Barons' Cave' at Reigate Castle was, naturally, where Langton and the conspirators met. Names from the story were adopted for the large, new houses being built in the area; the new owners of 'Weycliffe' near St. Catherine's re-named it 'Langton Priory'. However, the idea that the tale was the work of an established author rather reduced its mystery and excitement, and soon it was being referred to as a 'legend'. Dozens of local guidebooks and magazine articles written since have quietly dropped any reference to Martin Tupper and merely say 'According to tradition . . .' At least this has the merit of putting *Stephan Langton* back into the realms of unreliable history. As in the case of the Chertsey Curfew Bell, historical fiction becomes a legend when the author is forgotten.

So what are we to make of all this? Some might argue that Tupper gave people an interest in local history that they might otherwise not have had. This is a dangerous argument. History that is not true is not history. Once an attractive, romantic falsehood has taken root, as with the Pilgrim's Way, it can never be eradicated — 'bad history drives out good', in that respect. So if you go to the Silent Pool, shed a tear — not for Emma the woodcutter's daughter, but for historical truth which lies drowned there.

The Guildford Massacre

Guildford, the county town of Surrey, lies in the gap cut in the North Downs by the river Wey. It was founded by Saxon settlers during the 5th century after Christ and by the mid 900s it had become an important regional centre. Despite its age, however, Guildford has only once played a prominent part in English history: an unenviable part as the scene of one of the worst acts of treachery and cruelty ever committed in this kingdom.

The background to the story is tangled, and biased records make it difficult to be certain of the true facts. Its origins lie in the complicated relationships between the sons of Emma of Normandy. She had married Ethelred the Unready, King of England from 979 to 1016, and had two sons: Edward, later called the Confessor, and Alfred, called the Atheling or Princeling. After Ethelred died, Emma married his successor, the Danish king Cnut (or Canute), and had another son, Harthacnut. However, King Cnut already had a son, Harold Harefoot, by his common-law wife Elfgifu. Before Cnut himself died in 1035 he had nominated Harthacnut to succeed him. Harthacnut had his hands full, though, fighting to protect his lands in Denmark and could not afford to leave in the middle of such a crisis. As a temporary measure, then, Harold Harefoot was appointed as acting ruler until his half-brother was free to ascend the throne. However, Harold was the man on the spot, and had as good a claim to the crown as Harthacnut as Danish law recognised his mother's relationship with King Cnut as legitimate. He declared himself King Harold I.

Queen Emma's eldest sons, Edward and Alfred, viewed these developments with concern. They supported the Norman faction in the English court, and indeed they had been exiled in Normandy since their father Ethelred's death. The Scandinavian faction of Harold was now in the ascendant, and Alfred the Atheling decided to intervene. It is possible that he wanted to talk to his mother Emma personally. What he intended to say to her will never be known – perhaps a protest over Harold's claim to the throne, or a reminder of Emma's Norman roots and the rights of her eldest son Edward. In any event, he gathered together a retinue of courtiers and attendants, and set sail across the Channel. It was the last voyage that any of them were to make.

Landing on the south coast, Alfred was met by Godwin, the wealthy and influential Earl of Wessex and a central figure in the power politics of the English court. The Atheling knew Godwin to be a close adviser of his mother and the two men greeted each other in all seeming friendliness. Certainly Alfred would be taken to see Queen Emma and naturally he would be escorted by a number of English soldiers fitting for a visitor of such importance. The company set off inland, Godwin perhaps riding and chatting with Alfred, the Norman and the English soldiers marching side by side. At the end of the day's journey they came to Guildford, where there was a royal residence — a suitable place to rest and spend the night. It is said that a feast was served in the great hall, Godwin and the Atheling sitting together in the place of honour and their followers eating and drinking in all good fellowship. If tradition was observed, the feast would have ended with long narrative songs, telling tales of ancient heroes. Eventually the tired travellers thought of sleep and, following the usual practice, they bedded down in the hall itself, around the open fire that smouldered in the middle of it.

Many never woke again. In the middle of the night Godwin's men, as secretly arranged beforehand, rose stealthily from their pretended sleep and fell on their erstwhile drinking companions. Swords and battle-axes rose and thudded down, hacking and slashing at the startled and defenceless Normans. Screams and prayers for mercy rent the peaceful night air, but no mercy was shown. Those not killed at once had their hands tied behind their backs and were led out to be butchered or sold into slavery. Alfred the Atheling was tied up and blinded. He was sent to Ely, where he died of his injuries.

News of the massacre shocked the whole of Christendom. Similar acts of cruelty were not unheard of at this time, but the betrayal of the traditional rules of hospitality was considered monstrous. The Normans nursed the grudge, and paid it back in full at the Battle of Hastings thirty years later. It is still uncertain why Godwin acted as he did – or even if he did, for some accounts throw the blame onto King Harold. It may be that Godwin thought that, by killing the Atheling, Harold's claim to the throne would be strengthened. On the other hand, Alfred's elder brother had the major claim to the throne and it is hard to see what the murder could achieve except to spark off a bitter feud. Whatever the reason for it, the massacre at Guildford was a cause of embarrassment and remorse to the Scandinavian faction at the English court. Harthacnut, who became king when Harold died, chose Edward the Confessor to succeed him, perhaps as some way of making up for the cruel murder of Edward's brother.

Nearly nine hundred years later, in 1929, building work on the Mount above Guildford uncovered some human bones. Archaeologists subsequently excavated the remains of nearly two hundred bodies, hurriedly buried in shallow graves, tumbled in together, hands tied, heads, arms and legs hacked off and carelessly tossed in. It may very well be that these were the mortal remains of Alfred the Atheling's unfortunate companions. The grisly story is tersely recorded in the *Anglo-Saxon Chronicle*. 'Alfred the innocent prince wished to visit his mother, but Godwin stopped him and made him captive. His comrades he scattered; some they laid in bonds, and some they blinded, some they mutilated, and some they scalped. No bloodier deed was done in this land.'

The Vicar of Warlingham's Fairy Cures

Disease was an ever-present threat to the people of old Surrey, as everywhere else, and a threat that was not properly understood even by the medical profession. Qualified doctors, moreover, were rarely found outside large towns, and the majority of country people could not have afforded their fees even if they were nearby. In this respect the poorer patient was lucky; the bleeding and purging that were the standard remedies of the trained physician often did more harm than good. Instead there were others who could be consulted; apothecaries in the market towns who both sold and prescribed drugs, 'wise women' or 'wound charmers' in the villages who made a side-line of medical advice and treatment, and, cheapest of all, traditional family remedies in the home. To a large extent the cures offered by all these, both professional and amateur, were herbal. The recipes, indeed, were esteemed more highly the more ingredients they contained and the more elaborately they were to be prepared.

It is fashionable now to maintain that country people in the past knew more about herbs than modern doctors do, and that these remedies had active properties that are still efficacious today. This, sadly, does not accord with the evidence. Not only was there no agreement between the herbalists as to which plant cured which disease, they often made such ludicrously extravagant claims for their effectiveness that one wonders why anyone ever died. Regrettably, widespread infant mortality and frequent fatal epidemics show just how little herbal medicine really had to offer.

An important element in folk-medicine, in addition to herbs, was magic. As well as — or instead of — drinking preparations or applying poultices, set rituals were employed. The treatment must take place at a certain time and perhaps certain actions must be gone through, or certain rhymes repeated. The similarity of these to witches' spells was not lost on contemporaries. Often, deliberately Christian phrases or features were adopted to reassure the patient — and any suspicious onlookers — that this was thoroughly 'white' magic. All these characteristics can be illustrated from the medicines recommended by the vicar of Warlingham in the 16th century. Like many householders, he kept a notebook of many dozens of medicinal recipes. The difference about his, however, is that he claimed they were taught to him by the fairies.

The first is a good example of a Christian rhyme used as a healing charm. To stop a wound bleeding you must recite

> There were three Maryes went over the floude;
> The one bid stande, the other stente bloude:
> Then bespake Mary that Jesus Christ bore,
> Defende gods forbod thou shouldeste bleede anye more.

The vicar does not note whether *anyone* could employ this rhyme, or only a 'wound-charmer' who had a reputation for special powers of healing.

Toothache has always been a particularly trying form of pain, but the vicar is ready to deal with it. 'To make an akeing tooth fall out. — Take wheate meale, and mixe therewith the milke of the hearbe called spurge, and make thereof past or douge, with which ye shall fill the hollowe of the tooth, and let it be there a certayne time, and the tooth will fall out of it selfe. Allso, if you wash your mouth and teethe once a month with wine wherein the root of this hearbe hath bene sodden, you shall never have payne in your teethe'. Washing the teeth with wine would be an expensive procedure for most countryfolk, but no doubt a popular one. Neither were cosmetic problems ignored. 'For him that hath naturally a red face. — Take foure ownces of the kyrnells of peaches, and three ownces of gorde seeds, and make therof an oyle, wherewith you shall annoynte his face morninge and eveninge; this will kill and destroy all redness. A thinge founde true by experience.' The last sentence rather implies that some of the others have not been. Even the ravages of time can be reversed. 'To remedye baldnes of the heade. — Take a quantitye of Suthernwoode, and put it upon kindled coales to burne; and beeing made into powder, mix it with the oyle of radishes and annoynte the balde place, and you shall see great experiences.' Disappointingly, the good vicar does not go into details of the great experiences that might be expected. There is a straightforward way 'to make the face fayre. – Take the blossoms of beanes, and distill them, and wash the face in that water, and it will be fair.' How simple the vicar made it all sound!

A particularly encouraging means of raising depressed spirits goes as follows. 'To comforte the braine. — Take and drink one ounce and an half of rosewater mixed with white wine, both comforteth and strengtheth the brain, and maketh it courageous, and comforteth all the substance of the harte'. One might argue that the white wine *without* the rosewater would have the same effect. Over-indulgence of that nature, though, is also catered for. 'For one that is or will be dronken. — Take swallowes and burne them, and make a powder of them; and give the dronken man thereof to drinke, and he shall never be dronken hereafter.' This can scarcely be called a herbal remedy, however, nor is it clear whether powdered swallow-ash contains some powerful anti-intoxicant or whether a drunkard once made to drink it will simply make sure he is never made to again.

Hidden amongst all the rest is one cure that sums up the strengths and weaknesses of folk-medicine. 'A medicine against all manner of infirmities. — Take and drink a cupfull of the juice of betonye, the first Thursday in May, and he shall be delivered from all manner of diseases for that yeare.' If such a simple procedure could prevent all ills, what was the purpose of all the dozens of other recipes in the vicar's book? Indeed, if this or any of the remedies against infectious diseases had been effective, then European history would have been very different. But it is too easy to mock these superstitious cures. They at least enabled the patient to feel that something was being done for him, and doctors are now realising how important the patient's attitude to his disease is to his recovery. If the country people truly believed these cures would do them good, then they might very well have done so.

The Rabbit Woman of Godalming

Mary Tofts was born in Godalming in 1701 and married Joshua Tofts, a poor cloth-worker, when she was 19. In the normal way of things, she had three children, but then she was suddenly lifted from the obscurity of her impoverished rural life to be for a few weeks the wonder of the nation — as the Rabbit Woman of Godalming.

According to her own account, Mary Tofts was working in a field near the Ockford Road one day in April 1726 when she was surprised by a rabbit. Soon afterwards she fell sick with stomach pains and was obsessed with a craving for rabbit-meat. She exhibited signs of pregnancy, and in November the time seemed near. John Howard, a 'man-midwife' was called from Guildford and was present at the birth, so he said, of a litter of rabbits. He immediately informed an acquaintance of his, Nathaniel St. André. St. André was Swiss and had come to England as a dancing-master and fencing instructor, but had developed an interest in anatomy. Because he spoke German he was appointed by the German-speaking George I as his anatomist in 1723. His medical career prospered and he became a surgeon at the Westminster Hospital. On hearing the news of the miracle, St. André hurried down to Guildford, where Howard had installed Mary Tofts in lodgings opposite his own house. Soon after St. André arrived on the 15th November she began to go into labour once again and two more rabbits were born before his very eyes.

The surgeon hurried back to London to write a pamphlet recording the unnatural births, which caused a storm of horror and amazement when it was published. Preachers saw this as a fulfilment of prophecies in the Bible, and rabbit-meat became suddenly unpopular. Mary Tofts, and of course her ever-present adviser John Howard, became famous overnight and soon the whole country was talking of the wonder. The ladies of the court were disturbed by the thought that they might give birth to monsters, and it may have been Queen Caroline who urged an investigation of the affair. Cyriacus Ahlers, a German surgeon at the court, went down to Guildford on 20th November. He alone, and not his companion, was allowed into the room with Mary Tofts and Howard, who insisted on answering for her when Ahlers attempted to question her. Soon she began yet again to show signs of an approaching delivery and at length produced several pieces of a dead rabbit. Howard prevented Ahlers from getting too close, however, and both he and Mary Tofts behaved very furtively.

However, Ahlers kept his suspicions to himself, even when Howard asked him to suggest to the King that she, and of course her medical adviser, should be given state pensions. Ahlers returned to the court in London convinced that a fraud was being perpetrated and told the King as much. St. André felt that his reputation was at stake and called in to support him a man whose expert opinion was more influential than Ahlers'. Sir Richard Manningham was the leading gynaecologist of the day, and all the fashionable ladies sought his help at childbirth. He was a Fellow of the Royal Society, and also a qualified physician – which Howard, St. André, and Ahlers were not. St. André invited Manningham to Guildford on 28th November, where he examined Mary Tofts and witnessed the apparent birth of several more pieces of rabbit.

He was unconvinced, and accused her of faking. She burst into tears and St. André argued that he was mistaken: all was genuine. Manningham proposed that she should be moved to London where other experts could be consulted and the next day she put up in a hostelry near what is now Leicester Square. Conveniently, labour pains began promptly, and continued for several days with no result. She was visited by several courtiers and others interested in the case, and she must have been desperate to satisfy them of her good faith. She secretly asked the hotel porter to get her a rabbit, but he immediately went to tell a local magistrate,

Sir Thomas Clarges. In vain she protested that she only wanted to eat the rabbit. Clarges arrested her, and would have taken her off to prison if Sir Richard Manningham had not intervened.

Keeping her under surveillance, he repeatedly urged her to confess. If she was lying, he said, then her accomplices would soon betray her. If she truly had given birth to rabbits, then she must undergo a drastic operation to make sure she had no more. On 7th December she confessed. It had all been a hoax, supposed to gain her and her attendants money. An enquiry held locally by Lord Onslow heard evidence from a witness who claimed that Joshua Tofts had bought two rabbits from her days before the first miraculous birth, and had hurriedly tried to buy more when St. André had been in Guildford. Mary Tofts was convicted of being 'a vile cheat and imposter' and spent some time in Tothill Fields prison. She was released and back in Godalming by February 1728, however, when she gave birth again — this time to a human baby.

St. André's reputation was ruined, and he became a laughing stock. Caricatures and libellous pamphlets mocked him as 'the dancing-master' and denounced him as a quack. After a brief notoriety, though, the stir subsided and the affair was forgotten. Forgotten, that is, outside west Surrey. The people of Guildford, always ready for a joke at Godalming's expense, were delighted by the whole business, and for years afterwards would yell 'Godalming rabbit!' at any unfortunate townsman they met. Some were so brave as to make mewing noises like a rabbit or a cat when in Godalming itself. The joker had to be a good runner, though, for he risked being chased out of town by the enraged inhabitants. Mary Tofts herself died in 1763, in the poverty and obscurity from which she had briefly emerged as the Rabbit Woman of Godalming.

The Godstone Witch

The fear of witchcraft haunted country people well into the present century. Why this should be so is unclear. Both the educated and the uneducated unquestioningly believed in the existence of witches and the evil effects of their spells in Elizabethan and Jacobean times. Witchcraft, indeed, was a criminal offence punishable by hanging (not by burning at the stake, incidentally: that was a continental habit). But the last witch to be hanged in Surrey was Elizabeth Hatton of Dorking in 1655. From then on the authorities became more sceptical about accusations of witchcraft, and magistrates were increasingly reluctant to convict. In 1736 the crime of witchcraft was abolished and, as far as the educated were concerned, it ceased to exist.

Not so amongst the country labourers, however. Traditionally, witches had been blamed for diseases in children and farm animals in particular and the educated sceptics were unable to offer any convincing alternative explanation. Just as folk-medicine employed magic charms to ward off illness, so the malevolence of witches could be averted by certain rituals. An old iron blade or a stone with a natural hole in it hung over an animal's stall will protect it, and a horseshoe nailed round the stable keyhole will prevent a witch flying in. Pins play an important part in breaking spells; stuck into a suspected witch's footprint, she will jump with pain if she is guilty. Stuck into a door-jamb, pins will prevent a witch entering. Amateur witchfinders would offer advice on these and other methods of detecting and avoiding witchcraft. A sprig of hellebore might be recommended, to be stuck through the ear of a bewitched pig, and sycamore was a useful wood for keeping spells away. Willow, on the other hand, must be avoided, and never used as part of a horse's harness. If a secret payment could be made to the witch without her suspecting it, then her spell would be broken. Perhaps the most elaborate and impressive way of curing a bewitched person was to make a witch-bottle. This involved taking a bottle, often a German stoneware wine-bottle of the type nowadays called a bellarmine. This was filled with a mixture of water, hair, and nail-clippings from the sufferer, and the inevitable pins added. The bottle was stoppered, and heated — often by being buried under the hearth. As the contents boiled, so it was believed that the blood of the witch would boil also. These bottles are sometimes found by people renovating old cottages in Surrey, bricked up in the fire-place.

In the stories, witches were nearly always women, frequently widows, nearly always old, and almost always very poor. Often they would live in a humble cottage away from the rest of the village, feared and avoided by the neighbours. It did not need much to earn a poor old woman in such circumstances the reputation of a witch. An outburst of bad temper would be enough, or one of the often-repeated anecdotes of witchcraft could be told about her.

Some of these anecdotes can be illustrated from Godstone. Just to the south of the village is a narrow lane now called the Enterdent, but known as Polly Pains Bottom in the middle of the last century. Here dwelt an old woman who was said to be able to turn herself into the shape of any animal she wished. On one occasion it was a dog, who frightened a team of horses pulling a hay-waggon, which overturned and was wrecked. Another time it was a cat. A passer-by picked up an attractive black cat in Polly Pains Bottom and carried it along for a while. However, the further they walked, the bigger and bigger the cat grew. A friend met by chance was horrified by the size of the creature; witch's work, undoubtedly. The cat was quickly returned to the spot where it had been picked up, getting smaller and smaller until it vanished into thin air. In 1862 a strange hare was noticed in the vicinity when odd things happened, and the villagers decided that the hare was a witch in disguise. A pack of hounds was organised to hunt it, and they set off one day in hot pursuit. Before they could seize it, however, the hare escaped down a drain. One dog did manage to bite its back leg, though — and the next day the old lady was seen walking with a limp.

This story of a hare (often a white one) being wounded and the suspected witch limping the following day, is told in villages all over southern Surrey and, of course, the counties around. An attack of rheumatism must have been the cause of many an old woman being branded as a witch. The interference with the team of horses is typical too. If a waggon got stuck in a lane, witches were held responsible and various means were employed to break the spell. A knife blade could be passed under each horse's hooves, for example, or a notch cut out of the spokes of a wheel. Alternatively, the horses' necks could be whipped, as it was well known that witches could become invisible and sit astride the horses' necks, knotting the manes for stirrups. It hardly needs to be pointed out that there are perfectly straightforward reasons why a waggon should stick fast in the clay lanes of southern Surrey. However, if people feel frustrated or threatened it is only natural for them to seek someone to blame for their troubles.

A common feature of stories like the ones from Godstone is that the suspected witch need not be present at the scene of her supposed crime — at least not recognisably. This would make it hard for the accusations to be refuted. The resulting reputation could be a serious matter for the old woman. She would be isolated from the rest of village society, and even be savagely assaulted in the belief that drawing blood from her would break her spells. Some old women may have taken a mischievous pleasure in being thought to have supernatural powers, but surely to most it was another burden added to their already difficult lives. It must be acknowledged that this injustice was one of the less attractive aspects of the old country way of life.

Woking and the Necropolis

In the 1840s the people of London were dying at an unprecedented rate. For one thing there were many more of them than there had ever been before, and for another the cramped and insanitary conditions in the crowded slums led to epidemics of such deadly diseases as cholera and typhoid. These took a dreadful toll, particularly of the poor, and posed the grim problem of where to bury the corpses. The graveyards of the London churches were laid out when the population was tiny compared with the numbers now swelling the metropolis. Furthermore it was recognised that the over-crowded churchyards were themselves a threat to the health of the neighbourhoods around. Accordingly burials in London churchyards were banned in 1850 and alternative arrangements were considered. A cemetery was required near London, with convenient transport, and preferably where land was cheap, for it would have to be a very large cemetery. Attention turned to Woking.

Woking was a small village beside the River Wey, but the speculators were more interested in Woking Common, a large area of heathland to the north and west. The soil was too poor for farming, but perfectly suited for digging graves . . . or building houses. The railway which crossed Woking Common had been built in 1838 and Woking Station stood in the empty heathland a mile and a half from the village. What could be more convenient? Here was a large expanse of infertile, and therefore cheap, land, with a direct rail link to London. All that was required was a company to exploit it. The London Necropolis and National Mausoleum Company was formed in 1851. The impressive word 'necropolis' — city of the dead — was taken from the great burial grounds of ancient Egypt, and the Company sketched out grandiose schemes for a vast cemetery serving the whole country. The next stage was to acquire the necessary land. A bill was introduced in Parliament to give the Company the power to purchase and enclose the land at Woking by agreement — or compulsion if agreement failed. Henry Drummond of Albury, M.P. for West Surrey, expressed grave doubts as to the motives of the Company. This was nothing more nor less than a fraud, he maintained. Under the pretence of setting up a cemetery, the Company were going to be empowered to buy up large acreages of land — far more than was needed. This surplus land, with its convenient station, was just as suitable for housing development as for burials, and Drummond foresaw that most of the land acquired would be later sold off for building at a handsome profit. The Earl of Onslow was lord of the manor of Woking, and he had been offered £35,000 for the commons. However, there were others whose interests were involved. Tenants and other local inhabitants had the right to graze animals on the common and cut turf for fuel. Many of these people were poor, and these rights and privileges were very important to them. Drummond feared that they would suffer when the land was enclosed. However, a clause was introduced into the the bill to compensate those who would lose their common rights, and another that prevented any surplus land being sold by the Company without Parliament's approval. Drummond appeared to be satisfied and the Act was passed in 1852. The Company acquired the whole of Woking Common, some 2,300 acres — representing a quarter of the whole parish, in fact. Despite the assurances made, however, there were arguments over the compensation for lost common rights for three years before another Act of Parliament settled the matter.

At Brookwood, on the western edge of the parish, work began on the cemetery. Paths were laid out, trees and shrubs planted, and chapels built for different denominations. Plots were reserved for certain London parishes, and later there was an area set aside for soldiers of various nationalities. With great ceremony the Brookwood Necropolis was opened by the Bishop of Winchester in November 1854 and burials began. The railway was crucial to its success and the London & South Western Railway provided special hearse carriages. The rigid class distinction that marked Victorian life is one of its least attractive features, and this distinction continued even after death. The L&SWR varied its fares: 'For each corpse of the pauper class 2s.6d., each of the artizan class 5s.0d., others £1.' Special trains left from the Company's own station near Waterloo every day, and a branch line ran right into the heart of the cemetery, with two stations. The Brookwood Necropolis became fashionable, and the venture was clearly a success.

However, Henry Drummond's initial suspicions were fully justified. The Necropolis only occupied 400 of the 2,300 acres originally bought, and soon the company was asking the government's permission to sell off the rest. It is curious that Drummond was silent during the short Parliamentary debate that followed. Suspiciously silent, one might think. A lot of money was at stake, and the few who raised objections were smoothly reassured. All that was intended, said Lord Redesdale, was to dispose of 'certain detached portions of land . . . which could never be properly appropriated to the purpose of a cemetery.' One might reasonably ask, if that was the case, why had they been acquired in the first place. The off-hand reference to 'certain detached portions' concealed the fact that over 80 per cent of the total was involved. Still, despite doubts of the Company's good faith, they were given the benefit of the doubt and the Act was passed. As one would expect, the area around Woking Station was considered the most suitable for development, and the Act that permitted the land sales stipulated that a church and a school should be built there. This clearly suggested that a new settlement was envisaged as growing up on the heathland around the station. This is indeed what happened. After a slow start, the area became gradually built up and within fifteen years people were referring to the original village as 'Old Woking' — 'Woking' itself was now the busy and expanding town around the station.

1879 brought a threat, albeit a distant one, to the Necropolis Company. The Cremation Society's crematorium was built at St.

John's. It was not until 1885 that the first legal cremation in Britain took place there, despite the objections of local clergymen. From then on there was an alternative to burial. Cremation, though, did not become widely accepted until the 1920s, by which time the Brookwood Necropolis had lost a great deal of its initial popularity. An air raid in 1941 destroyed the Company's station near Waterloo and the direct railway service was not revived after the war. Brookwood Cemetery is now somewhat overgrown and has a neglected air. The true monument to the London Necropolis and National Mausoleum Company, however, is the town of Woking itself: a town built, if not by fraud, then by some pretty sharp practice.

The Chertsey Curfew Bell

In the tower of the parish church of Chertsey there hangs a mediaeval bell. It is said to have come from Chertsey Abbey, which had stood nearby until Henry VIII turned all monasteries and abbeys into empty ruins. Around this ancient bell was woven a story that has since become famous throughout the English-speaking world.

Albert Smith was born in Chertsey in 1816, and grew up opposite the church, taking an interest in the bells there. Originally groomed to follow his father into medicine, Smith found that he had a natural talent for writing. Satirical essays and novels flowed from his cheerful pen and he became a popular author, scoring particular successes with his public readings of travel stories. His first play *Blanche Heriot, a Legend of Old Chertsey Church* was performed at the Surrey Theatre in 1842. The plot was a good one.

Blanche Heriot is a beautiful Chertsey girl, Queen of the May, in fact, but her heart is not in the merry-making. Her lover Neville Audley has gone away to fight with the Lancastrian army in the Wars of the Roses. However, the Lancastrians are heavily defeated at the battle of Barnet, and Neville flees to Chertsey to take leave of Blanche before escaping abroad. The victorious and vengeful Yorkists are hot on his heels, alas, and they run him to earth in Chertsey Abbey. Neville claims sanctuary there, but the Yorkist soldiers threaten to come and take him by force, with whatever consequences for the monks and their abbey. To avoid any harm to his hosts, Neville offers to give himself up to be beheaded, if only the soldiers will wait until the curfew bell tolls from the parish church that evening. This is agreed, and in the precious

83

hours remaining, Blanche sends a messenger to the King for a reprieve. Neville, it transpires, had chivalrously spared the life of an important Yorkist during the battle, who had given him a ring as a token of his gratitude. If Neville ever needed his help, the ring would ensure that it would be granted. Accordingly the messenger gallops off to the court with the vital ring, in the knowledge that he must return before the curfew or his journey would be in vain. Unfortunately he is delayed and as the hour of the curfew draws near Blanche realises that she must intervene herself if Neville is to live. But how? As soon as the bell rings out, he will be led out to the executioner's axe. The curfew bell, then, must not ring. Blanche runs to the church tower and climbs the dusty spiral stair, then up the ladder that leads to the chamber where the bells hang. Using all her strength, she throws down the ladder behind her to slow down any pursuit, then, just as the sexton below pulls on the rope, she flings herself onto the clapper of the curfew bell. She is swung to and fro, battered and hammered against the heavy metal of the bell, but she clings on with grim determination, her body deadening the sound. Curfew does not ring. Angry voices below indicate that the Yorkists are coming up to investigate, but then shouts and cheers in the street outside let her know that the messenger has at last returned with the reprieve. Neville is released, and marries the loyal girl who muffled his death knell with her fair young body.

The tale was well told in the rather stilted 'Olde Englishe' style that was so popular in historical romances in early Victorian times. It was full of local references and realistic detail, although Smith was unaware that mediaeval bells were not swung on wheels as they are today. The story became well-known locally, and quickly became established as a 'legend' — after all, was not that what Smith himself called it? Sixty years later another writer felt able to claim that 'the play in its outline follows the legend'. Of course it did: the play was the legend, and there is nothing to suggest that the story was anything more than the work of Albert Smith's imagination.

His play inspired at least two poems: Clifford Harrison's *The Legend of Chertsey* and Rose Hartwick's *Curfew must not Ring To-*

night. It was Rose Hartwick's version, written in 1867, seven years after Smith's death, that made the story famous. She changed the heroine's name to Bessie and her lover's to Basil Underwood. It is Cromwell who grants the pardon in this instance, and Rose Hartwick has the bell-ringing sexton being so deaf that he doesn't realise the curfew is not ringing. The poem is well-written after its kind and the repetitive line 'Curfew must not ring tonight!' is an impressive punctuation in the narrative. The poem spread the 'legend' far and wide on both sides of the Atlantic, although Chertsey itself was not mentioned. The unlikelihood of even the deafest sexton being unaware of even the lightest girl clinging to his bell seems not to have bothered anyone!

The 'legend' became even more distorted in the popular song *Hang on the Bell, Nellie* written by Connor, Erard, and Parker in 1948. This time the heroine was Nellie, whose father had been sentenced to be electrocuted — 'They didn't have a sofa, so they sent him to the chair.' The execution was to be when the curfew bell rang. True to form, Nellie muffled the bell and the reprieve came. Again there was no reference to Chertsey and the song treated the 'legend' with a certain lack of respect.

'Hang on the bell, Nellie, hang on the bell,
Your poor Dad is locked in a cold prison cell,
As you swing to the left and you swing to the right
Remember the curfew must nevah ring tonight.'

The curfew bell, a relic of days when the fires had to be covered at night — *couvre feu* in French — is still rung in the evening at Chertsey. The 'legend' is often told, usually in Albert Smith's version, though he is rarely given the credit for inventing it. The idea that this was an ancient folk-tale that Smith merely dramatised is an attractive one, but there is nothing to support it. As with Stephen Langton and the Silent Pool, we can answer the question 'When does historical fiction become a legend?' with the answer 'When the author's name is forgotten.

The Battle of Dorking

The pride of Victorian Britain was crushed by the Prussian army at the Battle of Dorking and her Empire lost in the humiliating surrender that followed. That, at least, was the claim made by the author of an article in *Blackwood's Magazine* in May 1871. At that time all Europe had been stunned by the ease with which the Prussians had defeated the French. Paris had surrended in January of that year after the humiliation of the incompetent French army and a bitter siege. The anonymous author felt that Britain should be warned that she, too, was vulnerable.

The story supposes that the army and the Royal Navy are scattered overseas fighting colonial wars. Prussia, having occupied France, then invades Denmark and Holland. Britain feels compelled to go to war with Prussia in their defence. The small fleet that has been retained in home waters is swiftly defeated, however, by a deadly new invention — the torpedo. The Channel is now clear for the German army to land at Worthing. Few regular soldiers are left in England, and so the Militia and the Volunteers are mobilised. The Militia were the forerunners of the Territorial Army, and the Volunteers were semi-independent associations of mainly middle-class civilians who enjoyed rifle-shooting and dressing up in uniforms. The Volunteers were viewed with undisguised contempt by the military authorities, who regarded them merely as civilians playing at soldiers. What followed was to emphasise their shortcomings.

The story is subtitled *The Reminiscences of a Volunteer* and is told from the view-point of a city clerk called hurriedly to the colours and sent down by the train to Horsham. But the Prussians are already in Horsham, and his regiment has to march back up onto the commanding heights of Leith Hill. The enemy's rapid advance threatens to outflank them and so they retreat once more northwards to Dorking. Weary and hungry after their frustrating marches, the discipline of the Volunteers breaks down and a baker's shop is looted. They then march out of the town up onto the Downs near Denbies, opposite Box Hill. Between lies the vital gap carved by the River Mole through which the Prussians must pass to capture London. The battle for the Dorking Gap is hard and bitter. The withering rifle fire from the Volunteers holds back the Prussian onslaught for a time, but their flank is turned by an attack from left. Courage alone is not enough when pitted against the most disciplined and professional soldiers in Europe. The Volunteers break and fall back onto Ranmore Common, from where they retreat through Leatherhead and Epsom to Kingston. Here they take a stand once more, south of Surbiton station, but are once more defeated. London is taken and the resulting peace treaty strips Great Britain of her colonies and cripples her industry.

An outcry greeted this story when it appeared. The author was eventually revealed as Sir George Chesney, the head of the Indian Civil Engineering College near Windsor, and his obvious familiarity with every inch of the ground, together with a genuine skill for realistic description, added to the impact of this cautionary tale. It was a time when defects in the army were being widely discussed, and many people found the weakness of the Volunteer system quite convincingly demonstrated. Others, however, were outraged by this public display of shortcomings in national defence. The Prime Minister, Gladstone, spoke out against alarmism in Parliament. 'I should not mind this Battle of Dorking if we could keep it to ourselves', he said 'but unfortunately these things go abroad, and they make us ridiculous in the eyes of the whole world.' He went on to remark that alarmism resulted in unnecessary military expenditure. However, the popular imagination had been seized, and the fictional tale added impetus to the movement for army reform.

General Sir Edward Hamley also took heed of 'The Battle of Dorking'. In the 1880s he proposed a scheme to Lord Salisbury, who had replaced Gladstone. Confidence was low in the Royal Navy's traditional ability to defend our shores, and Hamley sought to establish land defences. The North Downs, he suggested, were a natural rampart shielding London from a landing on the South Coast. Accordingly he recommended a string of forts all along the Downs from Guildford through Kent to the sea. Strictly speaking, these were not true forts, mounting artillery, but protected storehouses and magazines which would supply tools and ammunition for a series of trenches to be dug along the crest of the ridge if invasion threatened. Known officially as 'Mobilisation Centres', twelve of these were built in the 1890s. The one on Box Hill was intended to be a genuine fort with guns, and the contrasting vegetation in front of it still shows where the trees were felled to clear a field of fire. Others were built at Denbies, for example, not far from where the imaginary volunteer had stood, and at Henley Grove above Guildford. But, as Gladstone had predicted, they were a complete waste of money. The forts were obsolete in design before they were completed, and were never occupied except by caretakers. The launching of H.M.S. *Dreadnought* in 1905 re-established the Royal Navy as the indisputable master of the seas, and the government sold the useless forts back to the original landowners.

This was not quite the end of the influence of 'The Battle of Dorking'. In the summer of 1940 there was a far from imaginary threat of German invasion. Hamley's defence line was reconsidered and the North Downs again become a fortified barrier protecting the capital. Large, circular pill-boxes sprung up along the southern slopes of the chalk and sand ridges, and a huge anti-tank ditch marked the 'Stopline' beyond which none of Hitler's panzers was to pass. Churchill became Prime Minister at this point, however, and thought little of a plan that virtually abandoned Kent, Sussex, and half of Surrey to the invader. He insisted that the Germans should be held on the beaches, and the 'Stopline' became a part of a more extensive defence in depth. The concrete pillboxes and the earlier forts remain to this day as reminders of the Battle of Dorking, the most important event that never occurred in Surrey.

Secret Tunnels

There is something mysterious and appealing about secret tunnels and, like ghosts, tales of them can be found in every part of the county. While these stories are widely believed, however, little thought seems to be given as to why these tunnels should have been built. Usually they are blamed on smugglers. A good example is the shaft leading down from the wine cellars under Victoria Terrace in Dorking. Steps go down deep into the earth and end at the bank of an underground river, complete with a sunken boat said to have been used by smugglers to row secretly to the river Mole.

Many of these tunnel stories have a grain of truth in them, like the sand in an oyster, around which the fantasy is constructed. A good example of this is the short tunnel built by John Evelyn through the hillside at Albury Park towards Shere as part of his garden landscaping. The story grew up in the centuries that followed that this led over 17 miles to Carshalton, and that an army had once marched through it! Perhaps the most common discovery that starts off secret tunnel tales is that of Tudor drains. These were brick-lined and often large enough to allow a man to pass down them to clean them. One, for example, led from the now-vanished Byfleet Manor to the river nearby, and the tunnel discovered at Baynards Station near Cranleigh, and supposed to link the Manor with the Park, is probably another Tudor drain.

A legitimate reason for tunnelling is to dig out minerals, and imagination has extended and elaborated these old workings. In Reigate, for example, there is a network of tunnels and caves dug to obtain the fine silver sand used in the past for blotting ink and scattering on flagstone floors. The tunnels, however, are rumoured to connect the Priory with Reigate Castle, and a large excavation under the castle has been named the Barons' Cave, and is supposed to be the scene of a secret meeting of barons conspiring against bad King John. The same kind of exaggeration has happened at Guildford. Under part of the castle there run mediaeval chalk mines that very probably supplied the hard chalk used for the castle buildings. Usually called the Caverns, these were open to the public before the last war but were later closed and sealed off as unsafe. These and other old chalk workings in the town have given rise to tales of a fantastic network of tunnels running to places all over the surrounding area. If all were true, then Guildford would have a better underground system than London. The most persistent story is of a tunnel linking the castle with the Friary, passing through the two mediaeval undercrofts on either side of the High Street. No positive trace of this has ever been revealed, however.

This story is typical in that tunnels are very frequently supposed to link castles with the nearest monastery or priory. A large water conduit running down Castle Street in Farnham may have prompted the idea that an underground passage ran from the castle to Waverley Abbey over two miles away. There is no castle near Newark Priory, which stood by the river Wey near Ripley. The myth-makers had to invent a convent at Ockham, and relate how the canons of Newark dug a tunnel under the river so that they could have clandestine, and romantic, meetings with the nuns of Ockham. The river, however, burst through the roof of the tunnel and drowned the lustful monks. Slanderous tales such as this were common at the time of the Reformation, put about to discredit the old church and particularly the monks. Surely, though, the people at that time would have known there was never a nunnery at Ockham? The tunnel said to connect the monastery at Chilworth with the nunnery on St. Catherine's Hill is doubly untrue — *neither* establishment existed.

If the locality could not rise to a castle or a monastery, then the manor house and the church would have to do. Many tales are told of tunnels connecting the parish church with a house nearby, such as the Crown Inn at Chiddingfold, the old house at Tatsfield known as Colegates, and the Old Manor House at Caterham. Ancient or unusual buildings of any kind are likely to attract tunnel stories. The Obelisk at Camberley, for example, built by the notorious Regency rake Sir John Dashwood, is rumoured to be linked by a tunnel to the school at the bottom of the Knoll.

It is not unlikely that many of these rumours are started by wine-bins. These are alcoves built into the walls of many Georgian and Victorian cellars to store wine bottles at an even temperature. They often take the form of a shallow, arched tunnel leading off the cellar, and often are only a few feet deep with a rear wall of brick. It is easy to see how these could give the impression of a blocked-off tunnel.

The tales, though, are many and fantastical. The distances the secret passages are supposed to run are often incredible and the courses they take frequently pose difficulties even a modern civil engineer would find hard to overcome. Marshes, rivers, and soft sand ridges are regularly credited with subterranean passages. But the question rarely answered is why these tunnels should ever have been built in the first place. A great amount of awkward work is needed for even a short tunnel and a smuggler sweating away in a mile-long burrow might reasonably have asked himself whether this hard labour was worth the easy money he hoped to gain by it. Smugglers, love-sick monks, and anybody else would find it easier to make a secret journey overland by night. Nevertheless, secret tunnel stories are told, and will doubtless continue to be told as part of the rich folklore of Surrey.

The Tiptearers

The Twelve Days of Christmas were the longest holiday the farmworkers of old Surrey enjoyed, and there were many traditional customs associated with this time of the year. One of these was the tiptearers' or mummers' play. Details vary from place to place, but all the plays were basically the same. One by one the characters step forward and declare their identity. There is a fight between two of them and one is killed. A doctor is called who brings back the dead man to life. Other characters then enter and the play ends with an appeal for money or drink. The characters speak in doggerel rhymes. These were handed down by word of mouth to each new player with the inevitable result that they became garbled. For example 'The Turkish Knight' — often the villain — is frequently transformed to 'Turkey Snipe'. However, the words of all the plays bear such a close resemblance to each other that they very probably had their origin in a single, printed source — one of the cheap 'chapbooks' sold by pedlars in the 18th century. There are many who maintain the mummers' plays were the remnants of an ancient fertility rite or a memory of the Crusades but there is no evidence for this, other than wishful thinking. There is nothing to suggest that the mummers' play existed before the 1700s.

The players presented an impressive, not to say intimidating, appearance. Their costumes were covered with strips of paper or rags, which also hung from their weird headgear to conceal their faces. With their voices disguised, the audience might very well fail to recognise their friends and neighbours playing the parts. These parts usually included Father Christmas, Turkey Snipe, the Doctor and Saint or King George (sometimes updated to King William). Among others could be the Dragon, Billy Whittle, the Valiant Soldier, Beelzebub, and little Johnny Jack — 'with my wife and family on my back' (he had dolls hung all down the back of his costume). The anonymous disguise required each character

to announce his role. However, towards the end of the last century, the disguise was often abandoned and the characters dressed more the part: the Valiant Soldier in military uniform, King William with a crown, and so on.

The players were known as 'mummers' in the north of Surrey and 'tiptearers' (or tipteerers or tiptiers) in the south. ('Tiptearers' is an odd word — perhaps it may be related to the Scottish 'tappy teery' meaning 'topsy turvy'.) There would be between six and nine in each group, and they would meet some time before Christmas to rehearse, perhaps in a shed or barn. At Frensham in the 1870s they camped at Hammond's Wood, and the clashing of the wooden swords as they practised the fight could be heard half a mile away. From Christmas to Twelfth Night they would visit the farmhouses and pubs in the neighbourhood. They would rap on the door, fling it open, and the first line would ring out . . . 'In comes I, Old Father Christmas, welcome or welcome not . . .' One imagines they were always welcome, and the play proceeds as each enters in turn. There is a great deal of by-play and ad-libbing, perhaps exchanging banter with the audience; not, it may be assumed, of a particularly refined nature. One Turkish Knight used to hide a bag of red liquid under his coat, which burst when he was stabbed by St. George. This may not have been popular with the householders, however. Properties were few: wooden swords, of course, and the Doctor's bag filled with most unlikely medicines and instruments. The Giant Beelzebub might have a frying pan and a large club to encourage plentiful donations when he asked for them. Musical instruments were often carried, a fiddle perhaps or an accordion, and some performances included a jig or ended with carol singing.

There are references to the tiptearers from all over Surrey, but regrettably only four complete texts survive (from Frensham, Thursley, Horsell and Thames Ditton) although fragments are known from several other places. Together, though, it is possible to have a clear impression of what performances of the mummers' play must have been like in Victorian Surrey.

It must not be imagined that these were of a very high standard. The lines were chanted with little inflection and the actions owed more to slapstick clowning than tragic drama. George Sturt of Farnham, who was very sympathetic to the old traditions, found it hard to praise the mummers who visited him at Christmas 1897. 'I have to admit that as play-acting it was incomparably the very worst thing I have ever seen. In extenuation, I remember that it was extremely unlikely that any of the lads had ever seen any dramatic performance whatever.' Others were a little more charitable. A. J. Munby of Pyrford recorded that on Boxing Day 1883 mummers performed at his house . . . 'Half a dozen grown men, all wearing grotesque masks, strange hats, smocks or other guise over their clothes, all singing *God rest ye merry gentlemen,* most mournfully . . . I did not comprehend those vagrom men, but gave them a coin — as who should say, 'We may never see the likes of you again.'

Fortunately Munby's fears that the tiptearers would disappear forever were unfounded. By the outbreak of the First World War there were few to be seen, but in the last twenty or thirty years there has been a revival of the old plays in Surrey. These are often performed by Morris men, who do not normally dance in the winter months. So now the Christmas time customers of many a public house may once more be startled by the tiptearer's bold cry 'In comes I!'

Acknowledgements

My thanks to the distinguished naturalist Dr. Maurice Burton and the eminent folklorist Mr. George Frampton for material relating to the Surrey Puma.

Matthew Alexander